Convicted by Mercy

The Journey of Frank Simmonds
from the Streets to Sanctity

Edited by Mariangela C. Sullivan

Cover art by Jacquie Fankell

Printed in the United States of America

First Printing, 2019

ISBN, Paperback edition: 978-1-941457-13-9
ISBN, eBook edition: 978-1-941457-14-6

Human Adventure Books
123 Mesa Street
Scottsdale, AZ 00000

www.humanadventurebooks.com

Convicted by Mercy

The Journey of Frank Simmonds from the Streets to Sanctity

Rita A. Simmonds

HAB
Human Adventure Books

For Marshall, Wendi, Micah and Martin

Contents

Introduction 11

Preface 15

Barefoot in East New York 17

"My Mother Was My World" 19

"An All-Time Low" 25

"Lord, Show Me the Way" 31

"A Trap Door Opens Up" 41

"I'm Grateful just to Have a Pair of Shoes" 47

"Every Day Feels like Christmas" 49

"You Just Made My Whole Day" 55

"Climbing Mount Everest" 61

"The Biggest Mistake of My Life" 73

"God Put it in My Heart" 75

"You're Going to Walk Your Daughter Down the
Aisle" 79

"You're Going to See What Kind of Husband
I Am" 83

"I Just Got Real Deep with God" 93

"My Boy Can Go Anywhere I Go"...........................101

"No Son of Mine Is Going to Be Dressed
like That!" 107

"God Is Getting Ready to Ask Something Really
Big of Me" 115

The Doorkeeper..125

"I Have Everything I Need, Right Here,
Right Now" 139

"I Don't Carry the Cross; the Cross Carries Me" 147

"I'm Frank, Not Saint Francis" 149

"Suffering Has a Meaning"..161

"The Torture Never Stops" 167

"I Found Strength in Depending" 175

"Either He Exists or this Is a Big Scam" 179

Climbing Towards Calvary 189

"I'm Always Looking for How God Is Going to
Touch My Heart" 195

"I'm Still Living and Offering Everything"..............199

"That Monsignor Is a Funny Dude".........................205

"I Am a Changed Man" 215

"It's Not Hard to Love God"......................................221

"I Will Not Leave This World Hating My Wife" 225

"It's Not as Bad as it Looks" 229

"Time for the Treasuring"..231

"It's Not the End that's Coming; It's
the Beginning" 235

"You Don't Argue with the Truth" 243

"A Servant Leader" 249

Afterword 257

Tributes to Frank Simmonds 258

Introduction

Even now, years after his death, when I think about the harrowing things Frank went through, I still shudder: living on the streets, taking and selling drugs, crashing in crack houses…rats crawling over him, being dumped in a dumpster because "friends" presumed him dead.

To think of these things is all the more shocking because the Frank I first met…the tall, dapper, gentle-mannered, funny, other-directed, charismatic, handsome man…was so opposite of that.

Frank came into my life by way of one of my dearest friends, Rita Flansburg. She invited him to a performance of a play we were producing together. It was a brief meeting. But not long after, I shared a meal with Rita, and Frank, and friends in Brooklyn, and it was my honor to drive Frank home after dinner to his apartment in Harlem. Alone in the car for the forty-minute drive, here I began to get a sense of the exceptional humanity who was Frank Simmonds. I understood why Rita was attracted to Frank, and why she wanted me to get to know him better.

Frank's story is one of the most mind-blowing I have ever come across. If I didn't know the man in the flesh, I think I would have a hard time believing it was true.

But it is true…and so compelling that I knew Frank's story could heal a lot of people and save their souls. In 2010, I helped to produce an evangelization film for my

Dominican Province entitled *The God Question*. The gimmick of the film was to interview all sorts of people asking them the question, "Why do you believe in God? How do you know that God exists?" The cast of characters that stepped up to suggest an answer was impressive. But when we held a private, pre-release viewing of the film with a small group of trusted friends (people unafraid to give their criticism), one of my closest friends said simply about the film: "Frank is the best thing in it."

His interview took place at Coney Island. Frank is wearing a dark blue hooded sweatshirt. The camera is low, angled up at Frank. In the beautiful sunshine, Frank's face shows how much he is moved by the question. He is concentrating. He begins to speak:

I know that God exists because there is absolutely no other reason that I could possibly come up with for why I am alive today. I was a drug addict, you know—crack. I was out in the streets; I was running in the neighborhood where killing was normal. There was nothing—no ambition for anything other than just surviving the next minute. I really didn't have the skills to live that life. It didn't correspond to me, but I was bound by something...something that I didn't think I could ever break loose from. I never really thought that I would live to...I'm fifty-five today...I didn't think I would live to be fifty...I mean, the way I lived...and when you run out... [he chokes up] *when you put yourself in a position where you have to beg for your existence, that's when you realize that God exists. And I did just that, and he answered.*

I loved Frank. Everybody loved Frank. There's a million reasons why. But I think the main reason, the chief reason, the reason that cuts through everything and that unites people—the fans of Frank—with a bond unlike anything they ever experienced before, is because of this thing he said. He did, constantly, put himself in the position where he had to beg for his existence. And that's why he was so insanely happy. Most of us are not humble enough to live life from the position that we have to beg for our existence. And that's why we're so miserable and depressed. And discouraged. And alone.

But Frank showed us…and thereby taught us without ever intending to "teach" us…that putting ourselves in the position where we have to beg for our existence is the most reasonable way to approach reality. It was the secret to his infectious childlikeness. It is what made Frank such an awesome father. And it's why we miss him so much, and need his help from heaven. Because it's a scary thing to beg *every day* for our existence. It's a scary thing to depend on God and to trust him to answer. This is why the communion of saints itself exists: to give us the courage and confidence to live as beggars before God.

Fr. Peter John Cameron, O.P.

Preface

When I was eight months pregnant with my oldest son, I was driving around the streets of Manhattan looking for a spot where I could wait for my husband, Frank, who had gone into a store. I found one near a fire hydrant, and, as I prepared to back in, a young woman in a yellow sports car with a California license plate drove straight in behind me. Pregnant belly and all, I immediately jumped out of the car and confronted her.

She held her hand to her heart in disbelief: "Why are you yelling at me? I'm really a very nice person."

I apologized for my rash response, and she gave up the space.

When I relayed the story to Frank, he said, "I'da told her, 'Well, I'm *not* a nice person, so you better get out of that spot.'"

When I began writing Frank's story, I imagined that I would be telling the story of a saint. By the time I finished, I realized that my definition of sanctity had greatly evolved. Frank was a sinner, but he was also, as was said of him in an exhibit in Italy, "the face of mercy." His life highlights an important question: What makes us saints— our capacity, or God's mercy? I believe, after reading Frank's story, more people will realize their own call and possibility for sanctity.

Barefoot in East New York

One cold November night in 1998, Frank Simmonds went to the streets of East New York to buy crack. He had sold his coat and shoes, and used up all his money on drugs, but still needed to buy some more. He figured that he would have to rob someone, but who? It was two o'clock in the morning, and the streets were empty. He sat on the steps of an abandoned building, barefoot and shivering, hoping someone would pass by. Before long, he saw a man in the distance, walking towards him. Frank was getting tense, planning his attack. As the man got closer, Frank noticed that he was dressed in black with just a bit of white on his collar. It was a priest! Frank's adrenalin started pumping as he pictured the collection money in the man's pockets, but then he became disturbed at the thought of jumping and robbing a man of God. He decided that if the priest walked by without addressing him, he'd let him go; but if he said anything, Frank was going to rob him.

The priest passed by without saying a word, but when he got to the corner, he turned, looked directly at Frank, and said, "Young man, if you think God is going to come and lie down in the gutter with you, He won't. You know why? Because He's holy. But I will tell you one thing. If you call Him, He'll reach in and pull you out."

"You better get steppin' old man," Frank warned.

"My Mother Was My World"

Frank Antonio Simmonds was born on June 20, 1955, the youngest child of Christalia Simmonds and the only son of Francis A. Simmonds. His parents were born and raised in St. Thomas, Virgin Islands. Christalia had five children from previous relationships before she met and married Frank, Sr. He was younger than she, and from a well-to-do family, which disowned him when he married her. Frank was sixteen years younger than the next youngest sibling, Althea, and the only family member to be born in the United States, in Amityville, Long Island. Two months after his birth, on August 28th, the feast day of St. Augustine of Hippo, Frank was baptized in St. Martin of Tours Roman Catholic Church in the same city where he was born.

Frank's early years were happy ones. He was very well loved and never wanted for anything. Although his mother was strict, she showered him with affection. His father bought him expensive gifts. He was considered spoiled by his older siblings, who were raised in humble circumstances on the island of St. Thomas.

When Frank started school, he encountered his first experience of rejection. His large ears made him the object of constant ridicule, so much so that his parents paid for him to have plastic surgery. Frank recalled how he was not allowed to go swimming for an entire summer because he had bandages on his ears.

Frank had a special childhood friend, a little girl named Nina Gabriel. She was the only daughter of Frank and May Gabriel, who were friends with Frank's parents. Frank loved Nina. "She looked like an angel and had a very strong faith in God," he said of her. One day, when Frank was eleven years old, she told Frank that she was going away.

"What do you mean? Are you moving?"

"No," she said. "I'm going to be with Jesus."

Frank later found out that she was very ill and would soon die. He cried and cried. The next time he saw Nina, she was bed ridden.

"Aren't you afraid?" Frank asked her.

"No," she said. "I'm going to be with Jesus and all the angels."

Frank looked at her face. It was radiant. Nina died soon after. Frank never forgot how fearless and peaceful she was in the face of her own death, and still mentioned it as an adult.

Frank's parents were hardworking people. His father was a chemist who did research in a lab. He was a reserved, soft-spoken man who spent much of his free time reading. His mother was a registered nurse. She was vivacious, powerful and intensely loving. She drove a sports car and was a very fast driver. She loved to travel and to entertain. Their house was always full of music, drinking and dancing. "Come on, you fart busters," she would shout, "Let's get the party started!" This would send Frank's father running away to his study to read.

Frank's mother was the disciplinarian of the family and did not tolerate disrespect. When Frank was disobedient, he would hide under the bed, and his mother would find him with the end of a broom. Once, when he was a young teen, she responded to his back talk saying, "Oh, so you think you're a grown man? We'll here—" she wound up and punched him in the chest, knocking the wind out of him. "Mom didn't play," Frank would say. Still, his older siblings felt that, as the baby, he got away with a lot more than they had.

Frank was mischievous by nature, and a practical joker. "A mad scientist who would blow things up and laugh," says Althea. He liked to capture mice, frogs and other creatures, and frighten people with them. But he was also tender. Once he found a bird with a broken wing, and brought it into the house to nurse it back to health until it could fly away.

Frank shared a room with his older sister Emma's daughter, Dana, who was three years younger than "Frankie." Although technically Dana was his niece, they grew up together like brother and sister, and Dana was always either Frank's partner in crime, or the victim of his pranks. Once, he put photos of a dead uncle, lying in his coffin, all over the room and locked Dana in. From his bed on the top bunk, he would put a glove on a string and lower it down onto Dana's face while she slept on the bunk below.

Frank's father ran the biochemistry lab at Brunswick Hospital in Amityville. He often brought Frank and Dana there to show them around, explaining the work he did. They found it fascinating. At home they set up their own chemistry lab on the bar in the family room, and spent much of their time there. The family used to say that the pair were destined to become doctors. But Althea always pictured Frank as a lawyer because of his ability to "stand up to people and tell them what he thought, but not in a rude way. And he had answers for everything that you would ask him; he could always back up his story."

Frank loved baseball and had an extensive collection of baseball cards, which he often traded with Dana. Frank's father liked taking the two of them to Shea Stadium to watch the Mets play (though Frank would later become a devoted Yankee fan).

As Frank prepared to enter high school, his parents became concerned about the growing drug problem in their community. They also wanted Frank to get the best education possible. This prompted them to move to West Babylon, where they enrolled Frank in a predominantly white school. Again, Frank became the object of much rejection and ridicule, only this time plastic surgery wouldn't help. West Babylon High School in the late 1960s had only a handful of black students, and they were bullied every day. "Some of the white kids hung nooses on my locker or waited for me to use the bathroom so they could jump me and beat me up." The black students quickly learned that they had to stick together in order to survive. Frank felt frustrated that his parents did not understand that, in racist America, if you were black, you were considered to be less than those with white skin.

In 1970, Frank made his first trip to the Virgin Islands, with his parents, his older brother Kenny, who was a deaf mute, and Dana. Frank's maternal grandmother, Natividad (or Granny Nattie, as she was affectionately called) was advanced in years, and her health was failing. Frank, Sr., was very worried about returning to St. Thomas, as he was not on good terms with his family. Rumor had it that the Simmonds had put a curse on Frank's mother, but she insisted on going, so they boarded a cruise ship and set sail for the Caribbean. Frank enjoyed the trip. On the ship, his mother gave him a fifty-dollar bill and told him to go have fun. When they got to St. Thomas, Granny Nattie was bedridden. She held her rosary beads in her hand, praying the rosary over and over again, and when she met her youngest grandchild, she blessed him, making the sign of the cross on his forehead. She would die soon after.

On the way back to New York, Frank's mother became so ill that she was quarantined on the cruise ship. Shortly after their return, the cause of her symptoms was found. Frank would later recall the day his mother came to pick him up from summer school, and he saw an unfamiliar look in her eyes. "I always got this look of love that my mom gave me. This was a look of desperation."

She said, "Son, what are you going to do when Mommy's not around anymore?"

She revealed to Frank that she had been diagnosed with uterine cancer, and it had already reached an advanced stage. He told his mother to have faith; she would beat the cancer. Frank's parents had raised him Roman Catholic, and Sunday Mass was an important event in their house. His mother would wear her best dress with a matching wide-brimmed hat, his father a suit, with a flower in his breast pocket. Even though Frank hated all the fanfare and stiff clothing, he was a believer. He trusted that God was good and merciful, and he prayed ardently for his mother to be healed. But as the days went by, her health rapidly deteriorated. As her health declined, Frank later admitted to Dana, he began sneaking and taking his mother's pain medication. He was then a junior in high school.

"My mother was a 5 feet, 9 inch, 189-pound, strong West Indian woman," but the cancer made her unrecognizable. It pained Frank to see his mother sick in the hospital, weighing only 72 pounds.

Frank was a gifted athlete. He was unusually long-legged, willowy and very quick. He used to sign his name "FAST" (Frank Antonio Simmonds the Third). That winter, he won the high jump competition at school, and told everyone that he had done it for his mother. He couldn't wait to show her the medal. He raced home from school and told his father that he was going to the hospital with a surprise. Frank's father stopped him. "Your mother died this morning." It was February 1, 1973.

When Frank recalled his early years, he would say, "My mother was my world." He blamed God for taking her away. So, at the age of seventeen, he decided that God was of no consequence, and he turned away from his faith. He would spend hours and hours yelling at God in the basement of his house. "You're nothing but a statue or a picture on the wall!" he screamed. As Frank put it: "I lost faith in God at that moment. I chose not to be aware of God."

Frank had always had a stubborn, rebellious streak, but in his mother's absence, it took over his personality. He decided to go along with the climate of the times: "love and peace, and sex, drugs and rock and roll."

"An All-Time Low"

Frank found that drugs fulfilled two purposes. First, they helped him to fit in at school. He learned that no one seemed to care what color your skin was if you had drugs to share. Second, getting high helped to dull the pain of losing the person who mattered most in his life.

His father, who had depended on Christalia for nearly everything, lost control of his only son, and quickly remarried a woman with two young children, Veronica. He went to live with her in Amityville, leaving Frank, who was still in high school, alone in the family home in West Babylon. Frank had inherited some money from his mother's death, and with it he bought a sports car and turned the family home into a hangout, where his friends could come and get high. Frank's relationship with his father was complicated by the fact that he was not allowed in his father's new home because Veronica worried about what kind of influence he would be on her young boys. Frank's siblings were married and dealing with their own struggles. His sister, Althea, took their older brother Kenny, who was a deaf mute, to live with her in the Bronx, but Frank insisted on living by himself in West Babylon.

Frank soon dropped out of school, but he got his High School Equivalency Diploma a year later, and started working at a company that built grandfather clocks. He worked on a saw and used to get a lot of splinters in his hands. One day he decided to put gloves on, even though he was warned against it. As he was sawing, one of the gloves flew off his hand and hit the wall. He had cut his thumb, and it was hanging from his hand. When the ambulance came, he was sitting with his dangling thumb and forced himself to smile. "If I could smile at a time like this, I could smile through anything."

Fortunately, the doctors were able to re-attach Frank's thumb, although he would never be able to bend it from the knuckle again. He was given morphine for the pain, which helped to dull his emotional pain even better than marijuana. When his pain medication ran out, Frank's friend told him that heroine was just as good, so Frank started shooting heroine.

Frank's childhood friend, Bobby Ann, became his girlfriend. Eventually they moved in together and had a son, Marshall, born on November 26, 1978. But Frank's lifestyle was not well suited to settling down. He ended up fathering another child with a white woman from the neighborhood, Terry. Wendi was born on January 30, 1980. Frank visited Terry and asked if he could see his new daughter. "Can you promise to be a regular part of her life?" she asked. Frank didn't believe that he could. He went away sad.

Frank and Bobby Ann both worked in Farmingdale as electronic wirers. Frank loved the work, but couldn't advance because he was colorblind and had trouble identifying the wires.

Drugs were rapidly becoming the focal point of Frank's life. Soon heroin was not enough to satisfy him, so he added cocaine to the mix. While this combination allowed him "a more euphoric feeling, a better escape," it didn't last as long. Eventually, his arms were so scarred that he couldn't put needles in them anymore. That's when a friend handed him a crack pipe. "Crack took me to an all-time low. It took me to where I didn't care anymore about anything. All I wanted was another hit. It was like I was a walking zombie."

Eventually, Frank lost the family home that his father had left him to manage because he never paid the taxes. He moved into an abandoned house and fixed it up. His friends came and stayed with him. They smoked and drank all day and all night. "When you lose the awareness of the relationship with God, you lose hope. It's like walking in a dark tunnel with no light at the end – there's no direction, nothing. I stopped caring about anything."

Soon he was removed from that building. He took to the streets and wandered from one Long Island neighborhood to the next. "I was hiding out from my son. I didn't want him to see what I had become." One day, as he was wandering about, he saw two boys in the distance coming toward him. As they got closer, Frank realized one of them was Marshall. "I was in clothes that I had been wearing for three or four weeks, the same shoes that had been walking through puddles. I was a wreck."

Marshall was about ten years old at the time. He recognized his father and asked him to come home.

"I don't think your mother wants me around," he said.

Marshall told him that they'd seen his picture on a poster in the grocery store. Frank sometimes stole tee shirts from Pathmark. He would go into the aisle, rip open the packages and put a clean shirt on right in the store. The police would come and try to catch him. "Crackheads can't run," they would say, but Frank was an exception to that rule.

Frank was very upset and ashamed that his son had to see him in such bad shape. He apologized, but told him he had to go. Again, he walked away sad.

Frank started learning hard lessons about homelessness and addiction. One winter it was so cold that his feet froze, and he could no longer walk. He rolled down the hill to a "friend's" house and begged to come in.

"Do you have anything?"

"No." Frank knew he was referring to crack.

"Then you can't come in."

By now, Frank had been on the streets for nearly a decade, and his run-ins with the law continued. Some of the police officers felt pity for Frank. One told him, "We're not arresting you; we're rescuing you."

Others threatened Frank's life. On one occasion, he was picked up and taken to a cemetery, where some officers beat him for refusing to give them names of drug dealers. Realizing that he wasn't going to talk, they decided to shoot him and make it look like a suicide by putting a gun in his hand. Frank hugged his body tightly and rolled on the ground. The police became so angry they broke his jaw.

On December 18, 1988, Frank was arrested and jailed for selling drugs to an undercover police officer. He didn't mind going to jail because at least he would have regular meals and a place to sleep. However, selling drugs was a felony, and Frank hadn't thought about having to share space with other men serving time for serious crimes. Frank was 6 feet 2 inches tall but weighed only 130 pounds. "I was in there with hardened criminals. I was hardened and a criminal, but when you're in there with hardened, *hardened* criminals, then you know if you're a hardened, hardened criminal or not! These dudes' arms were big like my thighs."

Though drugs were passed around, Frank never indulged. In this prison environment, he preferred the consequences of not taking drugs to the agonizing fear and paranoia brought on by smoking crack. He also knew that he had to keep his wits about him in order to survive, and he joined a Bible study run by a Catholic chaplain for support.

"Lord, Show Me the Way"

One day, about a week before his sentencing, he was playing spades with a group of inmates, and began writing on the paper he was using to keep score. Before he knew it, he had written a poem. "It didn't come from my mind; it came from my heart." To Frank's surprise, it was a religious poem, which he titled "Lord, Show Me the Way." Frank was always able to recite it from memory:

I pray for a good future.
God, please overlook my past.
Forgive my sins so I can find happiness at last.
I am a lost sheep. Please lead me back to the herd.
Help me change my life, Lord; just bless me with Your Word.
I'm paying for my mistakes. Please, help me ease the pains.
Release me from the anxiety of my spirit being in chains.
I love you so much, God. Your Son dealt with pain and strife.
I'm thankful that Jesus, for our sins, has given up His life.
You're so understanding, so willing to forgive.
Please cleanse my mind and body so my spirit can live.
Reality has set in; I know I've done wrong.

My heart is filled with sorrow; it's for Your
forgiveness that I long.
I feel like I'm unworthy to ask You for this blessing.
You know it took me very long to have to learn my
lesson.
But I will not give up to Satan the life You've given
me.
Please send the Holy Spirit as my guide until I come
to Thee.

When Frank went to his Bible study class, he showed the poem to the chaplain, who asked if he could hold on to it. Frank agreed, and went to sit in the back of the room. The front seats were taken by the very intimidating inmates with life sentences. The chaplain read Frank's poem to the group. The men in the room were deeply moved. The chaplain asked, "Do you know who wrote it? The man sitting in the back." They looked behind them, surprised, and said to Frank, "Word? You wrote that poem? I need a copy of that!" The fame of Frank's poem gained him protectors in the jail, who called him "The Poet." As Frank recalls, "This is how God began to show me He would not abandon me."

When Frank went before Judge George F. X. McInerney for sentencing, he was so frightened that his knees began to shake. At that time, the Rockefeller Drug Laws, signed into law in 1973 by Governor Nelson Rockefeller, mandated at least fifteen years behind bars for possession and sale of drugs. The judge asked Frank, "Mr. Simmonds, are you aware that when you sell drugs you are contributing to an organization that is killing the youth of America?"

"Yes, your honor, but I'm not a drug dealer; I'm a drug addict."

"Mr. Simmonds, do you realize that, as a drug addict, you are still supporting an organization that is killing the youth of America?"

"Yes, your honor."

The judge then sentenced Frank to five to fifteen years in prison.

Frank imagined himself upstate with the hardened criminals. "They've probably got a wig waiting for me," he thought.

Then he noticed that the judge was reading something from his file.

"Did you write this poem?" he asked, holding up a piece of paper.

Frank's lawyer had given the judge a copy of "Lord, Show Me the Way."

"Yes, your honor."

Frank's lawyer then pointed out that his client was educated and intelligent, and he had demonstrated religious conviction and repentance for his crime. He added that Frank was not a career criminal yet, but if he were to be sent Upstate, he would become one.

The judge ordered Frank to complete a drug rehabilitation program, along with five years' probation. The prospect of prison time vanished.

Frank began treatment in May of 1989, at a facility called Daytop Village, Inc. in Far Rockaway, Queens. Daytop, which was originally an acronym for Drugs Addicts Yield to Probation, (later changed to Drug Addicts Yield to Other's Persuasion, and finally Drug Addicts Yield to Persuasion) was founded in 1963 by a Catholic priest, Monsignor William B. O'Brien, who was weary of blessing the caskets of heroin-addicted young people in the Bronx. At the time, the prevailing attitude toward drug addicts was that nothing could be done for them, and that they needed to be locked away in psychiatric hospitals or prisons, where they wouldn't be a menace to society.

Daytop used harsh methods to break the addicts down and make them take personal responsibility for their actions. They were encouraged to snitch on each other, something that Frank could never get used to. Group sessions went on for hours and hours, exhausting the clients' defenses. Many of the counselors were former addicts who were Vietnam vets or had done prison time. Their discipline tactics would soon come to be viewed as extremely unorthodox. Once, Frank was made to wear a sign around his neck that read: "Confront me about why I'm a liar." On another occasion, he was accused of acting like a baby, and was made to sit in a large crib, wearing only an adult diaper and a bonnet.

But Frank had great social intelligence and was a fast learner. Soon he was able to participate in some of Daytop's education programs. He became a student in their staff trainee program and a G.E.D tutor. He also wrote more poetry. Frank had a folder filled with poems, some typed, some handwritten, some with illustrations of roses, praying hands or the cross with a heart in the middle of it. Many of the poems were prayers. One was called "A Prayer for Strength":

Lord God Almighty, please listen to my prayer.
I am weak and in need of Your love, strength and care.
Deep inside of my body, my spirit is loving and good.
Yet I have not done the things that I know I should.
I want to live a life that is both pleasant and calm.
Even though I didn't live right, I meant no one any harm.
All around me in this world there is hatred and

violence,
so I'm praying to you for strength in total silence.
Our Father, in Heaven, please hear my prayer for
strength.
Whatever I must now sacrifice, I will go to any length.
Your glory reaches out to those in need of freedom
from the serpent.
Free me from these worldly temptations. I am Your
humble servant.
My prayer for strength from weaknesses, I ask of You,
oh Lord.
I'm unsure how many letdowns my poor soul can now
afford.
I love you, God in Heaven, and I'm now down on my
knees.
Help me see the light, oh Lord. Thank you. Jesus,
Please!

Other poems were strong cries for companionship, like
"The Apple of Love":

I've looked through the forest for a special tree,
a tree that bears a very special fruit of love eternally.
This fruit is very elusive. It's very hard to find.
Many men have looked before and went out of their
mind.
You may ask yourself, what could I be thinking of?
A tree that's far beyond your dreams bears the Apple
of Love.
What has taken over me? Can I be possessed?
I cannot give up my search. It's the key to my success.
No one else can help me. I must find it first.
I need the love inside this fruit to satisfy my thirst.
See, I am a very lonely man. I've been hurt many
times before.

35

I'm trying hard to pull myself up from the floor.
The love I had was always phony, rotten to the core.
When I thought that I was loved, someone closed the door.
I'm waiting for my mind to be in free flight like a dove.
I search time and time again for the Apple of my Love.

Frank was a man crying out for help. He also recognized that his lifestyle had caused him to hurt others. In "See" he writes,

See yourself as you get older
Tell the Lord what you have learned.
Is there weight upon your shoulder?
Are there bridges that you have burned?

In "Then Who Is to Blame?" he wishes to admit God's presence in his life, and accept responsibility for his faults:

There is a greater power that most of us know
that planted our seeds and watches us grow.
Let's prove God's creation was not made in vain.
If we're not open to change, then who is to blame?

He also desired to atone for the wrongs he has committed. In his poem, "Could This Morning Be the One?" he writes,

One day I will have paid the price
For the things that I have done.
Could this be the morning?
Could this morning be the one?

Frank's poetry did not go unnoticed. On July 3, 1990, Frank received a letter from one of his counselors.

Dear Frank,

It was so good to see you looking SO FINE! We are really proud of you, Frank.

As I read over your poetry, your struggle is very apparent. You've battled the drugs hard, and you've won. I believe they won't take you over again because you want so badly to stay clean. I suppose fighting against an addiction is a life-long battle. Cigarettes and food are my addictions. I have a dear friend (a priest) who believes that everyone battles some kind of addiction—his is work.

The problem sometimes is knowing just what an addiction is. I think it's any compulsion which gets in your way of living a full life—anything that limits your freedom, takes away your choices, sits between you and God. Perhaps I'm wrong.

You know how we all feel about you, Frank. You wormed your way into our hearts, and we found out we cared deeply for you. That doesn't happen with very many people who come to us, you know. You were special—somehow, we recognized your goodness. We always hoped you'd find some way to channel your incredible ability to charm people, and it looks like you have. You can either use your talent to love or to con others. You've obviously chosen to love.

Enclosed are copies of 3 of your poems. We will use at least one in the book of poems we're publishing for our "coffee house" we're giving in August. And, a young man, an actor who volunteers at Outreach, will read one or two of yours that night. Naturally, we will send you a copy of the book when it's printed.

Well, take care, Frank. Know we're praying for you.

Jo

While Frank was in treatment, he learned that his father had become ill. He went to visit him, hoping that the good news of his sobriety would boost his father's health. Frank told him, "You know Dad, I'm back. I'm your son again. This is the time where you and I are going to get back all the stuff that we lost."

Their relationship had suffered greatly in the years following Christalia's death. Although Frank was not permitted in his father's house, he would often show up at the Northport VA Medical Center where his father worked, and ask for money. Once Frank had a terrible toothache. His father gave him $300 for a root canal. Frank had the tooth pulled for $25 and spent the remainder on crack. His father had also bailed him out countless times when he got pulled over by the police for speeding, driving without insurance, driving with a suspended license, and many, many other vehicular infractions, until he no longer had a car to drive. Understandably, Frank's sobriety was a great relief to Frank, Sr. He was very proud. He said, "You know what? I have my son back."

On September 15, 1993, Frank received his Daytop graduation diploma stating that he "was a bona fide participant" and "did successfully complete each of the required phases." This included a work program, in which he worked for two years as a door monitor and therapy aide at an institute for persons with mental disabilities, the Institute for Applied Human Dynamics, in the Bronx. He received a letter of recommendation from his supervisor, Elizabeth Corrigan, dated May 25, 1993, which stated that he was "hard-working, trustworthy and reliable...in his dual capacity as door monitor and therapy aide." She explained that, "due to the nature of many of the behavioral problems of the mentally retarded population (including assaultiveness, self-abusiveness and runnners) as well as physical disabilities," being a door monitor was a very important job, "an exacting one with high responsibilities in ensuring the safe transition of individuals." As a therapy aide, she wrote, Frank showed "genuine care for the mentally retarded population" as well as "the ability to maintain good relationships with his co-workers and follow the directions of his supervisors."

From Daytop, Frank went to live with his best friend, Anthony Andrews, who had an apartment in South Ozone Park, Queens. A year later, he found a job in Brooklyn as a mental hygiene therapy aide at Kingsborough Psychiatric Center. Again, in this job, he was praised for being a hard worker and very personable. One of his supervisors described him as "dependable, conscientious, caring toward his patients and willing to accept and utilize criticism."

Frank's freedom from drug abuse had also opened doors in his personal life. One day he received a shocking phone call from Marshall about his daughter: "Dad, Wendi is here. She wants to meet you." Frank jumped in the shower, got dressed and boarded the Long Island Railroad headed to West Babylon, where Marshall lived with his mother and grandmother. Wendi was twelve years old and had been pestering her mother, Terry, about who her father was. She was surprised to learn that she had lived just three blocks away from her brother her whole life. When Frank arrived at Bobby Ann's house, he immediately embraced his daughter. "Now I know where I got my nose from," Wendi remarked. Frank was amazed at how much Wendi looked like his mother. It was a joyful reunion, which answered a lot of questions for Wendi, but also created new ones: why did she have to wait twelve years to meet her father?

Wendi's mother Terry had been in high school when she became pregnant, and Wendi was raised by her grandparents. Wendi's grandparents were Caucasian, and her grandfather owned a lot of guns. Frank feared for his life. Had Wendi's grandfather not been killed in a hunting accident when Wendi was in elementary school, this reunion may never have taken place.

Wendi tried to make up for lost time by sending Frank photos of herself throughout the years—school pictures, dance photos, pictures unwrapping Christmas presents and blowing out birthday candles. They would continue to keep in touch.

Frank was also making up for lost time with Frank, Sr., but, sadly, his father's health condition was getting worse. What Frank had feared all along was true: his father had cancer. He fought the illness for over five years, spending his final days in Brunswick General Hospital. Toward the end, he told Frank: "I just want to know, before I close my eyes, that I left a responsible son in the world."

Frank promised his father that he could die in peace. Then he spoke some words his father was not used to hearing: "I love you, Pop."

"A Trap Door Opens Up"

On February 9, 1996, Francis A. Simmonds's kidneys failed, and he closed his eyes for the last time. The next three years of Frank's life were his lowest. "Just when you think you've hit rock bottom and can't fall any further, a trap door opens up underneath you." When he went to the reading of his father's will, he was blind-sided. All of his father's assets were left to Veronica and her children. "I wish that I had had a relationship that I could have acknowledged at that point, because no matter what a program gave me, the pain came back. It came back worse." Frank once again felt lost and alone in the world.

One day, Frank was riding the bus, staring out the window, and he saw someone he knew smoking crack on the sidewalk. He got off the bus, and his seven years clean ended in an instant. He walked out on his job at Kingsborough Psychiatric Center and never returned. He took to the streets of East New York, a neighborhood he was vaguely familiar with because that's where he used to drive to from Long Island to buy drugs, and left his friend Anthony Andrews to pay the full rent of their Queens apartment. Once again he fell out of touch with everyone, including his siblings and children. At the time, he had a girlfriend, Edith, whom he also abandoned. His chief concern became finding money to support his drug habit. He would go to John F. Kennedy airport, grab a luggage cart, and transport people's luggage to their cars in the hopes of getting a tip. He washed windows at gas stations and stoplights. He slept on the subway. "I had gotten to a point where I didn't feel like I was a human being anymore. I wasn't brought up to be waiting for bakeries to throw out their old stuff so I could go into the dumpsters and eat, and to rob people, and try to go into the churches and steal the collection money while people were praying. This was totally against my nature as a person."

At times, Frank would overdose and have seizures in the street. Once his "friends" thought he was dead. They went through his pockets for whatever money or drugs they could find, and threw Frank in a dumpster.

Frank quickly learned that the streets of East New York were much harsher than those of Long Island. He had to be educated in order to survive. That's when he met his friend Earl Nixon, who lived in a makeshift shack made out of a refrigerator box at a gas station on Atlantic Avenue. Earl was an exception to "the word on the street—nobody wants you when you're down and out." He offered to share his home with Frank. Earl knew a lot about the streets. His nickname was "the Governor of East New York." He was willing to take Frank under his wing and mentor him. They forged a friendship much different from most of the conniving and traitorous relationships born from life on the streets. Though Frank and Earl were both looking to get high, Earl recognized something different in Frank. He called him, "My brother from another mother." Earl would later say, "I met Frank at a bad time, but the first feeling that I got was he was a good man, and he proved it… Frank was like an angel." Earl remembers that Frank was very fast moving, and did not stick around when trouble came. "He was the type of guy, he did what he had to do and moved on."

Still, Frank's life on the streets of East New York hardened him. He learned never to show weakness, and this sometimes meant hurting others before they could hurt him. "I was with the Atlantic Avenue crew, and the guys on Fulton... It was a whole different playing field. You had to do what everyone else does, or else you die, period."

What little faith Frank had in humanity had decreased to almost none. He entered crack houses filled with men having sex with other men in exchange for crack, women sneaking away from their husbands and children, selling themselves for the drug. He saw people who worked as doctors, lawyers, or businessmen by day, smoking crack with prostitutes at night.

During one of Frank's hustling ventures at the airport, he met Pastor Ben McKnight, who was working at a Volunteers of America outreach on Ward's Island. Ben offered to put a roof over Frank's head. Frank accepted, but the drug-infested shelter was not a place where Frank could get clean, although he did function well enough to become one of Ben's interns. Frank would stay at the homeless shelter overnight and travel with Ben to the various outreach locations during the day. Ben introduced Frank to David Burns, the director of the Volunteers of America satellite on the George Washington Bridge. Unaware that Frank was in the throes of drug addiction, David accepted Frank as his intern.

David was not used to the cruelty and hustle of the streets, but Frank was a veteran, and he became David's right hand. "Once we were out in the van," David would later recall, "and there were some guys milling around. Frank told me, 'Don't make eye contact with them.' He knew instinctively when people were up to no good." Not only was he quick and full of street smarts, but his suffering had made him compassionate, and his humor enabled him to disarm even the most difficult clients. And even though he was not able to practice what he preached in order to help himself, he was able to utilize what he had learned at Daytop to help others. As David's admiration and trust in Frank increased, so did the torture Frank felt over leading a double life.

After receiving his small stipend one cold November night, Frank went to the streets of East New York and met a man he would never see again—the priest he decided to rob. After telling Frank that God would never join him in the gutter, but would pull him up if he asked, the priest turned the corner. As soon as he did, Frank was on his heels, but when he reached the corner, the stranger was gone. The street was empty and silent, and there were no lights on in any of the buildings. He seemed to have vanished into the air.

At that, Frank became *convicted.* This was an expression Frank used throughout his life to describe defining moments of change. Once Frank was *convicted,* it meant he was open to change, and he never looked back. That night, Frank realized how far he had fallen. He saw himself no longer as a man, but as a werewolf howling at the moon, who remained a werewolf even when the sun came up. "When am I going to turn back into myself?"

He walked through the dark streets like a madman, yelling into the sky, reverting back to the conversation he started with God when his mother died: "You're not real! You're a statue! You like people to worship You, but You don't help anybody! Look what You've done to me! You've abandoned me again! Look at me! I'm a monster! They say this life You gave me is such a beautiful life—I don't want it! Take it back! You can have it! And if You don't take it back, I'll give it back to You."

He made up his mind to end his life by jumping in front of the subway train. But then something very strange happened. In the midst of his rant, a voice cried out from inside of him, and he heard himself say: "But God, if you stop me from what I'm about to do, I will serve You for the rest of my life." He shook his head in disbelief, "What?" This pronouncement, which passed through his mouth, seemed to have overridden his conscious mind. He would later recount that, at this moment, he became aware that he was in front of a Presence much greater than anything he had ever experienced before. "When my mother died, love died. But the moment after I uttered those words, I felt a love even greater than my mother's." Frank got down on his knees in the middle of the street. "My life flashed before me. In seconds everything that I had done raced through my mind... I went back to being a little innocent kid who used to play out in the street. I saw all of these things... My heart understood what was happening, but my flesh did not. It had no idea what was going on...but something totally corresponded to me at that moment, and I knew it was powerful."

Just then, he remembered that, some days earlier, he had been on the bus, and a man told him, "If you ever get in trouble, call this number: 1-800-WE-DETOX." And there just happened to be a pay phone right there on the sidewalk. Frank dialed the toll free number, and a man answered. Frank told him that he was a hopeless drug addict who was getting ready to commit suicide by jumping in front of the elevated J train.

"Where are you?" the man asked.

Frank told him that he was on Van Siclen Avenue and Fulton Street in Brooklyn. The man said, "A car will be there in fifteen minutes to pick you up."

"I can't wait fifteen minutes."

"Okay, we'll be there in ten."

"Ten or I'm jumping."

The car was there in eight minutes. Frank was taken to a hospital which looked very familiar to him. He asked one of the staff members where he was and discovered that the hospital used to be Hempstead General, where his mother had worked. Things began to make sense. He understood that his mother hadn't abandoned him. She had been praying for him all along. "I knew that it wasn't me. I knew that I was being given a gift. And my eyes were opened."

"I'm Grateful just to Have a Pair of Shoes"

My relationship with Frank began not long before this dramatic day. Although it began with just a few brief encounters, I deeply sensed from the beginning that Frank was destined for a life he was not currently living. Our first meeting was at the back of the auditorium at St. John the Evangelist Church in White Plains, New York. His boss, David, was a very good friend of mine. We had met in a theatre company, the Blackfriars, and were performing in a play about the life of St. Therese of Lisieux, *The Sacrament of Memory*, written and directed by our mutual friend, Fr. Peter Cameron, a Dominican priest. After the performance, David introduced me to Frank. Frank appeared clearly uncomfortable. He said a quick "hello," then told us he had to leave.

Some days later, on my way back home to Riverdale, in the Bronx, after teaching English as a Second Language in Harlem, I stopped by David's job, and there I saw a totally different Frank, cheerful and energetic among the people who came to him for help. He was having a conversation with a short, very round African American woman who told him that she needed a hug. Frank bent down, wrapped his long arms around her, and embraced her as if she were one of his own children.

"Frankie, remember my friend, Rita?" David was hoping that I could eventually introduce Frank to some of my friends in Communion and Liberation (CL), a Catholic lay community I belonged to which was founded in Milan, Italy in 1954 by now Servant of God, Monsignor Luigi Giussani.[1]

Frank turned toward me and told me that he was having a hard time walking in his new shoes. They were a donation to the shelter on Wards Island where he was staying.

"Maybe they need to be broken in," I said.

"No, the problem is that they're too small. But I'm grateful just to have a pair of shoes."

The next time I saw Frank at the George Washington Bridge, it was to invite him for dinner. It was November of 1998. David told me that he was going to Albany to be with his family for Thanksgiving, and asked me if I could invite Frank to my house. I was living in a house of consecrated women, called *Memores Domini*. We were a part of the CL community, but chose a life of virginity rather than marriage. The women in my house were more than happy to have Frank as our dinner guest. When I invited him, he started to cry. "It's been a long time since anyone's invited me into their home. I'm very grateful, but I'm sorry, I can't accept."

"Are you sure?"

Tears continued to fall from Frank's eyes. He said he was sure.

Frank had other plans.

---

[1] For more information about the Communion and Liberation movement, see its official website at https://english.clonline.org. For more information about Luigi Giussani, see a brief biography on the Communion and Liberation website, or see Alberto Savorana, *The Life of Luigi Giussani*, Montreal & Kingston: McGill-Queens University Press (2017).

"Every Day Feels like Christmas"

A couple days later, I received a distressed call from David. "Rita, have you heard from Frankie?"

"No. The last I saw him was at the outreach. I invited him for Thanksgiving, but he didn't accept."

"Well, he didn't show up for work today. He didn't even call. That's not like him. I'm very worried. Please pray."

I prayed a lot, and I asked all the women in my house to pray, too. Some days later, David received a call from Frank. He told David the truth: he had been smoking crack the whole time he was at the outreach. He'd had a life-changing experience on the streets of East New York, and was now in a rehab program, and he was determined never to use drugs again, but he needed time away to remain clean.

From Hempstead, he was transferred to a rehab upstate, and on January 5th, 1999, he entered a transitional work program in Harlem called Ready, Willing & Able. Frank described his first impressions in a December 13th radio interview with Bob Grant:

When I came through the door of the place, and I took a look at the gentlemen I saw inside, some of them I knew from the street, and they were...big.

They were...twice the size they were in the street. They were wearing gold. Some of them had on nice clothes, had cell phones...and I was like, really? This place can't be all like that. But when I looked inside, it was immaculate... They really treat people very well there...It blew all the myths and all the things I experienced from shelters...away.

At first, it was very hard for Frank to accept that the staff sincerely cared about him. He had grown accustomed to being abused and he was self-abusive. "When you're in the street, when people come up and try to help you, you think they want something from you, even though you have nothing to give...You don't believe that people care about you because you don't care about yourself."

When a counselor told him, "Don't talk to me like I'm your father—you're a man," Frank was surprised by his reaction. He had never even thought of himself as a man.

Frank described his experience of previous shelters. "I vegetated. I sat there and slept, ate, slept, ate, slept, ate, and nothing came of it...my life...just stayed the same." He went back to the streets because he felt "the street was just the same as being in a shelter." But Ready, Willing & Able required constant drug and alcohol testing, and gave the clients the opportunity to work, get paid, and pay rent. Frank was part of the street cleaning crew.

I was given all the equipment, thermal uniform...a broom and a can to push around...I had surrendered by the time I got to Ready. I was so fed up with the way I was living. They couldn't do nothing to me in that program that I didn't do worse to myself in the street, so when they gave me that bucket, I didn't mind. I went out there. I had Lexington Avenue, which was a very busy avenue in

front of Bloomingdale's. And I was the only one out
there singing and meeting all the people and saying
I was just thankful that I was still alive... Some
people that came out of the stores were like, "You
do such an excellent job...we're thankful." I made a
difference somewhere. I'm used to people running
from me and not even wanting to be seen by me.
These people were walking up and actually hugging
me in the street. There was no way that I couldn't
feel good about myself. I started getting stronger
and stronger, and it gave me a purpose in life. I
really thank God for it.

The radio interview came on the heels of a letter Frank
had written to the *New York Post* responding to an editorial
by Rosie O'Donnell chiding then Mayor Rudy Giuliani for
his way of dealing with homelessness. Frank's letter,
entitled, "Rosie, Work's a Way Out of Homelessness"
begins, "Rosie O'Donnell, give me a call. I can tell you
what it's like to be homeless. I can tell you why requiring
able-bodied people to work is being proposed in New
York City. It is sensible and compassionate." He then
described his life on the streets and in and out of rehab, up
to the day he planned to take his life.

He concluded by saying, "Work gives you your dignity
back. Work makes you part of life and lets you live on
life's terms."

A week or so after Frank entered Ready, Willing &
Able, I got his address from David, and wrote to him. I
sent him a Christmas card with a bronze medal of the
Blessed Virgin Mary. He later recalled that, when he
opened the letter, he was sitting in a room with two drug
dealers who were anxious to graduate from the program
and go back to the streets to resume business as usual.
Frank was so moved by the letter that he had to struggle to

control his tears. "I was astonished that, while I was still pulling myself together and had nothing to offer, someone cared for me."

From then on, Frank said that he put me "above all other women," alongside his mother. He added, "Even though I knew I did not deserve it, I was so proud to know her! Before, I could not trust anyone. Mind you, more than once my street 'friends' had thrown me into a dumpster, thinking I had died due to some seizures I was having at the time. I was garbage to them, and to myself."

Frank wrote me back almost immediately:

Dear Rita

*I thank you for being my friend and for being there
for me in times when most people want to jump off
of the ship. God will bless you for being the kind
and caring person that you are. I most certainly
keep you and David in my prayers and also in my
heart. I've learned a great deal from you and I
plan on passing it on to others in whatever ways
that God has enabled me to. There are not enough
words to express the gratitude that I have for being
blessed with meeting friends that I can actually feel
the goodness and warmth emitting from. I continue
to read your Christmas card over and over again.
It doesn't matter if you send all your letters on
Christmas cards because after meeting you, it feels
like every day is Christmas. God is doing
something with this whole segment of my life and
this time I am embracing His wisdom and love. I
love God, I love myself, I love you and I can't wait
to further strengthen our friendship. I will read
everything that you have sent me and study all I
can to find out the meaning of God's purpose in my*

life. I am lying down in my bed so please excuse my handwriting. Thank you for writing.

Love, Frank

It's interesting that he asked me to excuse his handwriting because the first thing I noticed was his beautiful script. And then, reading the letter, the tone was so gentle and sincere; I was moved. I wondered, who is this man? Where did he come from? What does he mean for my life? I read the letter to the women in my house. They, too, were moved. We all agreed that we should try again to have him over for dinner, but this time invite David, too. Frank would be more likely to accept if David accompanied him.

Fortunately, Frank accepted our dinner invitation, and he and David both came for dinner. My friend Olivetta Danese made pork ribs because David told me that's what Frank liked. We sat around our big dining room table and were amazed to discover what a great storyteller Frank was. When he told us about the sweet, shy little dog that had hidden under the car, but had bitten his nose when he went to rescue it, we laughed so hard, we cried. And that was just one in a series of stories that captivated us for an entire evening.

Though Frank was no longer working for David, they still found time to get together. I invited them to my English as a Second Language class in Harlem to talk about drug addiction and homelessness, and Frank won the class over with his engaging storytelling. The three of us sometimes met at a diner or coffee shop, and a couple times at Communion and Liberation events in Brooklyn. Once we went swing dancing at Lincoln Square with my friends George and Stacy Lugo, and my sister, Naomi.

That time, Frank seemed very uncomfortable. He left to call his ex-girlfriend, Edith, who was a swing dancer.

At this point, Frank's upward progress took another leap forward. Frank shared his conversion story with his friends at Ready, Willing & Able. One man challenged him: "You told God that you would serve Him for the rest of your life. What are you doing about that?" On the spot, Frank was convicted. He immediately began attending his friend, Pastor Ben McKnight's Pentecostal church in New Rochelle. On one occasion, Frank was among those invited to approach the altar to be prayed over. He stood in a row of people who, one by one, fell to the floor after Pastor McKnight laid his hands on them. Frank was determined not to fall to the floor unless his legs gave out. When Ben got to Frank, he asked him, "What do you want me to pray for?"

"Just ask God to give me whatever He thinks I need." After Ben's prayer, Frank remained standing. He walked away from the altar feeling the same as before.

A couple weeks later, his friend from the program remarked, "I see that you're different."

"What do you mean?" Frank asked.

His friend told him that he noticed Frank had stopped cursing and using foul language, something that was previously a part of Frank's every sentence. He also noticed that Frank no longer smoked cigarettes. Frank was surprised, but his friend was right. Without realizing it, Frank had quit his two-and-a-half-pack-a-day habit, and he had stopped cursing. Frank traced this transformation back to Ben's prayer.

"You Just Made My Whole Day"

While Frank's life seemed to be coming together, mine was beginning to fall apart. It was the year 2000, and I felt encompassed by a fearful and restless spirit. I had been a novice in *Memores Domini*, the consecrated lay group within Communion and Liberation, for nearly five years, and it was coming close to the time when I would have to decide definitively if this was my vocation. I wanted it to be, and yet I couldn't deny a growing emptiness inside. Getting up and going to work was becoming a chore, and being home in my room was excruciating. I cried constantly. My friends in the community tried to help. Eventually I went to see a psychiatrist who prescribed some anti-depressants, which sent me soaring out of control. I ended up doing a brief stint in a mental hospital. David kept in touch, but didn't know how to help. He told me that Frank was asking about me – would it be alright to share my situation with him? I told him, "Sure."

I remember getting a call from Frank right around Christmas time. He wanted to know why I hadn't told him what I was going through. "You help everybody out, but forget about yourself." Frank had graduated from Ready, Willing & Able, and was now working as a counselor in their After Care Program. He had a studio apartment in

Harlem and was very happy with his progress, but he gave all the credit to God. David and I went to see him in his new place. The walls were decorated with pictures of tigers, and a wooden bead curtain hung in the doorway. He was very proud.

At that time, I became very close friends with a man who would prove to be invaluable in my life and in Frank's life — Monsignor Lorenzo Albacete. He was a Puerto Rican theologian, a Roman Catholic priest, a scientist, and author of the book *God at the Ritz*. He wrote a column for the *New York Times* and was interviewed by Charlie Rose. His personality was larger than life, and he was very, very funny. He was one of the leaders of Communion and Liberation in the United States, and a wonderful companion at this difficult time in my life. When I was prone to search too deeply for solutions to my problems by studying the readings of our founder, Msgr. Luigi Giussani, he would tell me, "Focus on the ephemeral." To implement this advice, I remember going to see "Autumn in New York" by myself in the middle of the day. It was the perfect, sappy romantic movie for my grave mood.

Msgr. Albacete actually spoke about me when he went to Milan to see Fr. Giussani.

"Fr. Giussani asked about me?" I was amazed.

"Yes."

"What did he say?"

"He said, 'What's wrong with her?'"

"What did you tell him?"

"I said, 'I think she's had too much Giussani.'"

I was feeling less and less inclined to socialize. I quit my job in Harlem and was working only six hours a week, teaching ESL at a community college north of Manhattan. I was seeing a new psychiatrist, who prescribed low doses of three different medications. I asked him if I was bipolar. He said, "Well, you do have moods, but I think your problem is you haven't found your vocation." I couldn't bear the thought of leaving the women in my house. I had dedicated five years of my life to the *Memores Domini*, and I was in my mid-30s. If I left now I would have to start over with something new. I wanted to be settled already. Though the medication helped control my mood swings, I felt completely useless and lost.

In the spring of 2001, I was called for jury duty. The courthouse was on the other side of the Bronx, and I was not familiar with the area. On my way home, I took a wrong turn, and ended up driving over the Macombs Dam Bridge, heading into Manhattan! I was infuriated. How could I have made such a stupid mistake? I got off the bridge and drove right in front of the building where Frank worked. And there was Frank, coming back from the grocery store, with a bottle of soda in a plastic bag swinging from his hand! I couldn't believe it. I shouted out the car window at him. He stopped, and I pulled over. I jumped out of the car and we embraced. He ran to put his soda in his office, and then came out and sat in the car with me. We both felt that our meeting couldn't possibly have been a mere coincidence.

One of the first things I noticed was his shoes. He was wearing baby blue suede clogs. "I like your shoes," I said.

"Do they match? I don't even know what color they are!"

That's when I learned Frank was colorblind. I didn't think they matched, but it didn't matter. I was so happy to see him. He was happy, too.

"You just made my whole day," he said.

I felt like crying. It had been so long since I had made anybody's day. I felt like I was pulling everybody down. Who was this man who had so quickly pulled me out of months of feeling worthless?

At that same time, I received an email from my friend, Giorgio Vittadini, who was a very close friend of Fr. Giussani's and a leader in the CL community. He often came to New York from Milan to visit our house and the community at large, and to help us out. He and I had been corresponding on a regular basis, so he was well aware of what I was going through. In this particular email he told me:

Dear Rita,

Thank you for sharing this moment with me, but much more for your preference for Jesus. Don't worry: He always, always, always will find the way to reach you [...].

Please try to choose things that make you feel happy and light, that bring you joy because just God has to choose our cross (it is His business), we have just to choose Him through our joy.

Giorgio

That letter was all I needed to give myself permission to further my friendship with Frank. We talked on the phone every day. Frank became my closest friend and greatest confidant. At a time when I hated myself for how far I'd fallen, how useless I felt my life had become, in Frank I was met with complete and total acceptance. He liked me at my worst! And he placed no expectations on me. It seemed that the mercy he had experienced that night in East New York was for me, too. And Frank had a freedom and sincerity about him that I so desired for myself.

On April 29, 2001, my aunt, who had been sick for quite some time, passed away. My sister Naomi and I decided to make the trip to Cleveland, Ohio for the funeral and had to catch the Harlem bus to LaGuardia airport. I asked Frank if he wanted to have lunch with us before we left. He agreed, and met us at Sylvia's, a famous soul food restaurant on Malcolm X Boulevard. When the waitress came with our food, a sweet potato fell from one of the plates. Frank caught it in his hand. We were all amazed at his quick reflexes.

One day, I remember that I looked at Frank and thought, *what a great man. He would make a terrific husband.* I thought about fixing him up with someone, but who? He would need a woman who was very strong in her faith, but not in a moralistic sense. She would need to be able to constantly recognize and affirm the hand of God on him through the tremendous act of mercy he was shown, and not focus on his past life. She would have to have a good sense of humor and be firmly rooted in a community. A woman whose faith was weak or ungrounded, would end up succumbing to his lack of authority. Someone who was too pious would not be able to handle his past. I began to have the uncomfortable feeling that I was setting myself up.

Frank's friendship was drawing me in more and more. He was starting to look very strong and healthy. The day he got out of the elevator in his building, wearing a black sweat suit with a red dragon design on the front, was the day I knew my life had changed for good.

The first time I saw you for myself
you emerged from the elevator
in soft black sweats

59

with a dash of red
dragon breath
designed to stop me
in my steps.
I knew right then
I'm going down.
Your surface turned
my earth around.

Our first kiss seemed to terrify Frank. "We done bit the apple!"

I laughed.

"I'm not enough of a fool to mess with God's woman," he said. But Frank had never gone in for conventions. He didn't close the door on a relationship with me, despite how it might have seemed.

It was time for me to make a decision. Msgr. Albacete made it easier for me. He invited me out to dinner and told me that I could no longer live in the *Memores Domini* house. I could live in Brooklyn with my sister, Naomi, and come to Riverdale for house meetings. At that same time, a friend offered me a full time job at Kingsborough Community College in Brooklyn. Things were moving fast.

When Frank helped me move into my new apartment, I learned that he was very good at putting furniture together. We went to IKEA and bought a desk and end table for my new place, and Frank assembled them with great efficiency. Afterwards, we couldn't find the screwdriver. Naomi told me to call Frank; maybe he had taken it by accident. When I called and asked him, he became very upset, thinking that Naomi was accusing him of stealing. She had to talk to him to reassure him that she wasn't.

"Climbing Mount Everest"

My first house meeting living outside the house was my last. I cried the entire time. When it was over, I placed my key on the kitchen counter and left.

When I met with Giorgio Vittadini and Msgr. Albacete to make it official, Giorgio asked me flat out, "Are you in love with a man?"

"Yes." I said, still trying to recover from the question.

"Well, just make sure that he really, really, really loves you."

Later I met with my friend Chris Bacich, who was also in the *Memores Domini*. With a grave face he asked me, "Does this man know about your mood swings?"

"Yes."

"Well, did you ask him what he'll do when you have one of your episodes?"

"He told me that he'll go into the other room and watch TV."

Chris broke into a very loud laugh. "I like this guy!"

I fully expected Frank to be happy when I told him the news that I had officially left the *Memores Domini*. Instead, he became concerned. He said very frankly, "For me to be with a woman like you would be like climbing Mount Everest."

"But nothing's impossible with God," I told him.

Frank was starting to make a little bit of money. I thought he would be thinking about our future and start to save. I was disappointed when I discovered that he was constantly buying items which I considered unnecessary. He bought four formal suits and a lot of jewelry, not to mention the latest electronic items on the market. His apartment was so full of new purchases, there was barely room to walk.

One day I invited Frank to dinner with some friends from the Blackfriars Repertory Theatre group. Frank knew that we put on religious plays, and I think that's why he wore a crucifix around his neck, but this crucifix was unlike any I'd ever seen. It had a large, gold hip hop chain with an iced out Corpus and ruby-type stones on Jesus' hands, feet and loin cloth. I was extremely embarrassed, and made fun of his choice of jewelry. I later came to deeply regret it.

"Jeweled Jesus"

He wore a big gold chain
around his neck
with Christ outstretched in bling
across his chest—
studded sparkles marked His skin,
rhinestones where the nails went in.
Christ, be-dazzled in His pain—
blinding, kept away.

Though Frank had lived the life of a homeless drug addict, there was something about him that was completely innocent. I recognized an unworthiness in myself to be with someone who had been delivered from such horrible suffering and was trying to fit in and live a "normal" life. Frank just didn't fit in. In that necklace I recognized a great love that I couldn't fully embrace.

Also, Frank was forty-six years old, and had had several girlfriends in his life, but he didn't seem to know much about dating. Once he told me that his brother, Tony, was having a little get together at his house. "I'm thinking about going," he said.

"That's nice. You should go."

"You can come if you want to."

I think that was the first time Frank invited me anywhere. Tony had an apartment on the upper west side of Manhattan, where he was the superintendent of the building. Years before, he had run into Frank by chance, and had to ask him, "Is that you?" so altered was Frank's appearance from life on the streets. Two of their sisters, Emma and Althea, were also at the gathering that day. It was a joyous reunion. Frank had been lost to his family, and now he was found. Tony played "Hot Hot Hot," a West Indian-sounding carnival song by the Montserratian musician, Arrow. Tony was jumping around and dancing, Althea and Emma were laughing, and I was sitting on the couch next to Frank, who was all the while petting my hair. "I used to pet Mommy's hair like this," Frank told his sisters.

Tony gave Frank his old computer. Frank was thrilled. He had never owned a computer before, but he was very curious about how it worked. Frank brought the computer home, took it apart, and tried to put it back together again. When he had trouble, he paid people to come and work on it, observing them very carefully. Soon he was making computer repairs on his own.

I spent a lot of time watching him fiddle with his computer, or watching boxing or Yankee games with him. I quickly learned that we had two different ideas of what courtship should look like. Frank thought I was old fashioned in my thinking. "What are you, a doll? Am I supposed to just look at you?" I cried a lot, and Frank would get completely frustrated. Though we were in love, we didn't know how to be together.

One bright September morning, Frank called me at work. "A plane hit one of the Twin Towers, and it's on fire."

"What?"

Frank was watching the news. "Oh no! Another plane just hit the other tower!"

Our city was under attack. It wasn't long before both buildings had completely collapsed, killing over two thousand people. Frank was very worried about his sister, Althea, who worked just three blocks from the World Trade Center. I called all my family members and friends to make sure they were safe. The New Yorkers in the Communion and Liberation community gathered at St. Patrick's Cathedral, and Msgr. Albacete spoke. We were all in a state of shock, and, more than anything, we just wanted to be together.

It turned out that Althea was okay. When she saw the second plane hit from her office window, she grabbed her purse and ran out the door. She caught the last train leaving that area before transportation was shut down.

Frank was a great comfort to me during those frightening and sorrowful days. He helped me not to enter too deeply into the mystery of evil. When I expressed to him how disturbed I was by the reports of the people who jumped from the smoke and raging fire on the towers' upper floors, he told me, "We all saw them jump, but nobody saw God's Hand lifting them up as soon as they hit the ground." Frank was a man familiar with suffering and sorrow. He knew where to fix his gaze.

I came to love him immensely and to trust in and rely on his love for me. We didn't wait to have serious conversations about our future. He told me that he believed we would get married, but it would take some time.

"How long?" I was 38 years old and wanted to have children.

"Two years."

That seemed like a very long time. Frank was already having trouble with what he called my "rules and regulations." How would we survive two years?

I wrote a lot of poetry in those days, trying to make sense of our relationship. One I called "The Timed Eternal Way":

Love is a long, long way
My Baby,
Mysterious as a heart that's slashed
and laughs at how it bleeds.
Strange as a timed eternal need.
Love is a long, long way
my Baby.
It knows its own
and winds its path
where restless souls
can splash
then rest their wings—
beyond the nests
from fallen trees
where all are pleased
with beggars' hands
that always ask
(if they be true)
for more than what
a traveling man
alone
can do.

Love is a long, long way
my Baby—
a road that runs
not against nor from
but weathers windy days
though we try to grab
and shape in hands
this pleasure of
another state,
another kind—
and find the flesh
is but a sign—
My face and hair,
your fingertips
that seek to tap my Braille mind.
You learn we both have thought the same—
"The world that sees and then decrees,
in fact, is blind."
Yet what is mine
that won't decay?
And what is yours
that you can say
"It's mine"?
Love is a long, long way
My Baby,
and you have seen
my self at war
and how my nerves
are stretched and sore.
Is this the way?
The curving paths
that seem to force my feet
to stray?
Is your embrace

the place of peace
the way has made
for me?
In arms unarmed
I see your eyes
that see me safe
and seem to say,
"You're free to stop
and rest a while
and even fall
asleep,
my baby,
for love is a long, long way."
I wish to sleep
but not to fall—
I wish the freedom of before
yet know the taste,
the gnawing ache
of wanting less
for knowing more.
The fruit was plucked
before we came
from those who listened
to a voice
they knew untrue
and strange.
But things are not the same since then!
Things are not the same!
This long, long way of love we walk
has taken all our blame,
and still it begs and reassures,
"You're mine, and so with me remain."
Hold me to this road, my baby,
that holds us

though we stray—
the long, long road
that knows its own:
The timed eternal Way.

Suffering was built into our relationship, so radically different were our life experiences. I had always been an unapologetic, practicing Catholic, and actively sought to find my place in the Church. I had been in Mother Teresa's order of nuns, the Missionaries of Charity, for a year and a half after I graduated from college, and then, some years later, I had again tried to dedicate my life to Christ through poverty, chastity and obedience in the *Memores Domini*. Frank, although he was born and raised Roman Catholic, felt that the rules of the Church were man made, and was skeptical about its authority. He absolutely refused to follow anything that he didn't understand. His sister, Althea, had introduced him to Buddhism, but he would not chant unless he knew what the words meant. "How do I know I'm not saying, 'All Hail Satan!'?" Frank seemed most comfortable in Ben McKnight's Pentecostal church, or in the other Protestant churches where he played bass guitar in a band with his old friend Anthony Andrews.

I tried appealing to his Christian soul, in hopes of fostering greater unity between us: "Maybe we should ask Christ for help. When we're together, it's not just the two of us; He is with us." At times it seemed to me like Frank and Jesus were at opposite poles. I ended up walking out on him more than once, but always came back because I couldn't deny his love, which was so exceptional and sincere.

In October of 2001, I made an appeal in a poem I wrote, patterned on "O Captain! My Captain!" by Walt Whitman:

Oh Captain! My Captain! our trip has just begun,
The ship can carry any load but barrels bound to run,
The journey's long, the wind is strong, the gulls
surround us merry,
With wings like sails they try the gales, and tease what
seems to tarry;
   But wait! wait! wait!
      Are not mortals more than fowl?
         Though salty air excites our pulse
            New land will greet the bow.

Oh Captain! my Captain! we swing and sway - but
steer!
The very blue that moves us smooth can dash us to the
pier!
Or send us to a starless storm though chosen for the
race.
Where is the freedom of the task? Where are the
waves of Grace?
   Oh Captain and companion!
      This ocean throws your mate.
         How can I trust your hand and heart
            unless you steer me straight?

My Captain, will you answer? Your lips are close and
poised.
A crying wind invades my thoughts; one kiss will calm
the noise.
The ocean smacks a tender sound against our
starboard side.
The glow of moon speaks all too soon what evening
hopes to hide.
   Dear Captain, how this rocking boat
      knows well the way you breathe!

Sleep brief but dream eternal shores.
Wake up and take the lead.

Frank didn't seem to have my same concerns. He wrote me back:

You may have your issues.
I may not understand.
I keep a box of tissues.
I am your loving Man!

Frank was again back in touch with his children, and he had also become a grandfather. Marshall lived in West Babylon with his grandmother, his mother, his girlfriend, Tanya, and their baby daughter, Daezhana, just a couple houses down from where Frank used to live with his family. Wendi lived in Tennessee and was attending East Tennessee State University.

Frank continued to attend Ben's church in New Rochelle. They had become close friends. Ben learned that he could lean on Frank during difficult moments, and he was about to face one of his most difficult. Ben and his wife Beverly had three sons. Their youngest, Micah, was seven years old and had cancer. Frank had grown very attached to Micah and used to carry him around when he couldn't walk anymore. Frank told me, "He was like a man even though he was only seven. He had a maturity about him because he knew that he was going to die." Micah passed away on February 26, 2002. Frank told Ben, "If I ever have another son, I'm going to name him Micah."

Ben would later say about Frank: "When you meet a person like Frank, that person will always be in your life… Frank was a real person, genuine."

Very early on in our relationship, Frank told me that he had hepatitis C, which he traced back to the 1980s when he shared needles with other IV drug users. He had no symptoms, but there was no telling when they would appear. He assured me that the only way I could contract the disease was if his blood entered my bloodstream. New drugs were being approved to treat people with chronic hepatitis C. We had been dating about six months when Frank began interferon treatments, which caused him to become extremely ill. He lost a lot of weight and became very emotionally withdrawn. We spoke on the phone, but he didn't want to see me. When the treatment ended, the results were disappointing. Frank's condition had not improved, although there was no indication that it had worsened, either.

On March 19, 2002, Frank's brother Tony, who had been diagnosed with cancer when it was already at an advanced stage, passed away. Frank took the loss very hard. I was concerned and wanted to show my support. But when I went to Tony's calling hours, Frank introduced me as his friend, and acted like he didn't want me there.

We spent less time together. He had started working a second job and was tired all the time. When we did get together, he didn't want to go anywhere or do anything other than watch sports or an occasional movie on TV.

I spoke with Msgr. Albacete about everything that was going on in my relationship with Frank.

"Why don't you two just go out for a walk?"

"I've proposed that, but Frank always says he just wants to relax after working all day."

"I can't say that I blame him. I wouldn't want to go walking all around the streets after work, either," he said. Then he cautioned me, "Don't put too much pressure on Frank. It will be much easier for you to be a married woman than for Frank to be a married man." He told me to try to be patient.

I tried, but Frank was also pressuring me to have more of a physical relationship than I was comfortable with.

"Why can't you just marry me?" I asked.

"I'm not going to get married just because people think I should. I have to get married because that's what I really want to do."

Other times he told me, "It's not you that I'm worried about. I know you'd be a good wife."

Soon Frank got a new job working in the mail room for a business loan company in midtown Manhattan. His new boss, Bobby Tannnenhauser, hired men with criminal records who needed a second chance and were eager to work. Frank fit the bill. He became attached to Bobby immediately and had a great respect for him, and was excited about being in a professional environment where he no longer had to submit to random urine tests. At his new job, he also saw the possibility to advance to the IT department, where he could work with and learn from the men there who were highly trained professionals in a field he loved—technology.

"The Biggest Mistake of My Life"

I felt that Frank's new job, outside the addiction recovery world that he had seemed slotted for, was an extremely positive step, not just for Frank, but for our life together. Still, our relationship was riddled with constant stress and misunderstanding.

Frank and I started going out to dinner at a Chinese restaurant on East 86th Street. Inevitably I would start crying about everything that was wrong between us. Frank would get agitated and tell me, "Stop crying. People are looking at me like I'm beating you."

One day, Frank and I had planned to meet, but he told me to wait for him in the car. I was parked on Third Avenue in Harlem. He came to meet me, but stood on the sidewalk looking down at his feet. His hands were in his pockets. I rolled down the window.

"What's wrong?"

"I'm probably making the biggest mistake of my life, but I'm going to have to cut you loose."

"Well, if you know that it's the biggest mistake of your life, why are you making it?"

"This relationship is just too hard for me. You have too many rules and regulations. I'm sorry."

He walked away sad, and, of course, I was heartbroken. The pain was so excruciating, I didn't know what to do. I was still taking medication for my mood swings and I was afraid this was going to push me over the edge. I had been writing poetry and had had some of my work published. I decided that I would apply to Brooklyn College for a master of fine arts degree. I started dating other men.

Frank did not stop being a part of my life. He called me often, and always told me that he loved me. When one man I was seeing phoned and left a message on my answering machine, my sister, Naomi, told me, "When I hear this guy's voice, it makes me really miss Frank."

"I know," I said, "there's no one like Frank."

But I told myself that I had to move on. Frank and I were done. We could never be anything more than friends. Perhaps that was what he had wanted all along.

"God Put it in My Heart"

One day, I was driving north on the FDR Drive on Manhattan's east side, and I just turned the wheel and got off at Frank's exit. This time it was a deliberate wrong turn because I thought I just wasn't strong enough to stay away. I drove to his apartment building and rang the bell. He greeted me with great excitement. Just like that, we were back together again.

But our problems were right there waiting for us. Fearing yet another break up, I suggested something that I imagined he would quickly dismiss: "Maybe we can offer all this suffering to Christ and ask Him to use it to help us overcome our differences."

To my surprise, Frank became enlivened by the proposal. This was something that he seemed to understand much better than following "rules and regulations." We started to pray together, and he asked Christ to take our difficulties and use them to help us and to help others.

We went back to the Chinese restaurant on East 86th Street. I was very happy and wanted to talk to Frank about everything that was in my heart, but when I tried to initiate a conversation, he didn't respond. I started to cry.

"What's wrong now?" he asked.

"We have nothing to talk about. How are we ever going to get married?"

"You ask me a question right after I put food in my mouth! How am I supposed to answer you with a mouthful of food?"

I burst out laughing! I was beginning to see things in a different light.

And then one day, without any prior hints or warning, he told me, "God put it in my heart that you are my wife." And Frank was a man who lived not by rules and regulations, but according to his heart! He even said, "We don't even have to get married because you are already my wife." Of course, I objected to that, but in any case, from that moment on he treated me much differently. The change was palpable.

The first thing he did was go out and buy me a cell phone. "How can I have a wife and not be able to get in touch with her when I need to?"

The first thing *I* did was try to find a priest who would marry us. After two refused, too unsure about our commitment after so many ups and downs, I went with the obvious choice, Msgr. Lorenzo Albacete. The reason I didn't ask him to begin with was because he was very disorganized, and I was afraid the wedding would never happen. But he agreed to meet us almost immediately. Frank didn't understand why we had to see a priest at all. I told him that I wanted to get married in the Church, and the only way that that would be possible was if we took a marriage preparation course, or if we were accompanied by a priest. Frank chose the latter over the former, but he did not go into it with an open mind.

Our first meeting with Msgr. Albacete was in the Spring of 2003, at the parish where he sometimes said Mass, St. Mary's on the Lower East Side of Manhattan. When we entered the meeting room in the rectory, Monsignor was waiting for us. He was sitting in a chair, smoking a cigarette, and looking very relaxed and pleased. It was the first time the two of them had met.

"Frank, this is Monsignor Albacete," I said.

"Please, call me Lorenzo."

Frank was immediately disarmed.

"Ok, Lorenzo, we're here because we want to get married."

"Did you buy her a ring?"

"No." Frank answered.

"Well, she should have a ring."

"Okay," Frank said.

"Did you set a date?" He asked

"No." Frank answered.

"Well, you need to set a date, and this date can change. It's not written in stone. We'll call it a target date." Monsignor took out his calendar. I suggested October. We could get married on my 40th birthday, which was Saturday, October 4th. Frank agreed and Monsignor penciled in the date.

"Now remember, the date can be changed at any time."

The next day we decided to go buy my engagement ring. I got all dressed up and even put on makeup.

"What's all that about?" Frank asked.

"I'm excited," I said.

"Getting the Gold"[2]

Our love is like the smallest grain
that in the shortest spring
has given earth its golden sway,
while not withholding weeds.

---

[2] Rita A. Simmonds, "Getting the Gold," *The Remembered Arts Journal*, Weekly Edition, May 18, 2019.

They grew up with the tender wheat
that struggled from a seed
to stalks that stand the test of time
entwined in wily weeds.

To pull up weeds, we lose the wheat—
(both good and bad we've sown).
Yet summer keeps its promised heat
to mark and set for gold!

Frank and Msgr. Albacete became close friends in a very short period of time. Monsignor. was getting very excited about the wedding. "This is going to be great!" he said.

"You're Going to Walk Your Daughter Down the Aisle"

Not long after our engagement, my father had a stroke and was hospitalized. Frank and I decided to take a trip upstate to see him. It was the day before Easter. My father was unable to walk. Frank told him, "Pop, you're going to get out of that bed and walk again, because you're going to walk your daughter down the aisle." My father was moved to tears.

After the hospital visit, Frank didn't want to wait until October to get married. We moved the wedding up to July. Originally we were going to get married in Brooklyn, but because of my father's poor health, we decided to get married at St. Rose Church, the same church where I had been baptized and confirmed, in the small white, middle class town of Lima, New York, where I was raised.

Frank and I did not have a lot of money, so we decided the wedding would be a small one. Msgr. Albacete agreed to make the six-hour trip, accompanied by the women from the *Memores Domini* house, who were very happy and excited for me. Friends and family members came forward and offered their assistance: my sister Mary made the wedding invitations; her husband, Mike, offered to take pictures; our friends Cas and Valentina Patrick helped pay for my dress, and our friend Stacy Lugo took care of the flowers; members of the Communion and Liberation choir came and sang. My sister Naomi was my maid of honor, and my nieces, Lydia and Julia were flower girls, my nephews, Justin and Peter, ring bearers. My brothers Patrick and David were ushers, and my brothers Paul and Joe served on the altar. My friend, Raquel Isaza, did my hair and makeup, and my friends, Carl and Mary Anderson, offered their home for us to get ready in. My cousin Derrick Van Grol opened his home to Frank and his best man, Anthony, and Frank's friend, Curtis Walton, the videographer. My mother paid for the reception hall and the food, my sister Regina for the wine. My brother-in-law, Jonathan Fields, offered to play music, and my soon-to-be brother-in-law, Ken Genuard, to sing.

After the rehearsal, we had a big party at the American Hotel, one of the oldest establishments in Lima, famous for its homemade soup and "Speidie" sandwiches. Anthony played piano, Jonathan, guitar, and we all ate, and drank and sang.

Anthony and Curtis, Frank's only wedding guests, were amazed by the hospitality and openness of my family and friends. It seemed, for a time, that the racial walls that separated people had come down.

July 19, 2003 was the big day. Raquel finished putting the baby's breath in my hair and we were off to the church in Carl and Mary's black SUV. It was sunny but not hot. When we pulled into the driveway near the church, Frank, Anthony and Curtis were standing out front! My father was struggling to get out of the car. Curtis was filming, and Frank was shaking hands with my brother, Bill. "A great day for a wedding," he said, waving at the camera.

Frank went near the car door to help my father stand. "Come on, Pop!" They stood and posed for Curtis.

My father was moving very well considering he'd been unable to walk just three months earlier. But outside was not where the groom was supposed to be! Mary had to yell out the window to hustle them into the church.

"You're not supposed to see the bride!"

No one was more moved than Frank to see my father walking me down the aisle, since he had prophesied that it would come to pass.

Finally we stood before Msgr. Albacete, who was standing in front of the altar waiting for us. He said to Frank, "Are you sure this is what you want to do? If not, we can call the whole thing off right now."

Everyone laughed, but there was truth in Monsignor's humor. He knew how difficult it had been for Frank to get to where he stood. He wanted to make absolutely sure that Frank was there in complete freedom.

"This is what I want to do," said Frank.

For the second reading, I chose Romans 12:1-2, 9-18 because it reminded me of Frank, most particularly when St. Paul says, "Let love be sincere." Frank abhorred falseness and hypocrisy, and had no trouble telling people what he thought and felt, but he could always do this in a way that people were not offended. "Bless your persecutors; bless and do not curse them." He was also extremely forgiving, and prayed for his enemies. "Rejoice with those who rejoice, weep with those who weep. Have the same attitude toward all." Frank was very human. He could be as happy for people's successes as he could be sorrowful for their difficulties. He never thought he was better than anyone, and he didn't like people thinking they were better than him, yet he lived "peaceably with everyone."

During the homily, Albacete reminded us that, "for the Catholic Church, marriage is a sacrament, an event through which a human gesture becomes a means through which life triumphs over death, love over hatred, mercy over enmity, respect over manipulation, acceptance over rejection, inclusion over exclusion, fruitfulness over sterility; in short, being over nothingness." He added that, "if there is anything that absolutely characterizes Frank and Rita, it is the passion for humanity with which they have lived their lives… That relentless restlessness of the triumph of hope over despair has brought them here today, overcoming barriers that would have separated the less passionate."

We were at the top of Mount Everest.

"Dance for Two"

I love the chance I have with you
to bring my solo dance to two.
You're far from feet
that shuffle sweet
though you know my spin
from head to toe,
and so you grin
and turn me slow,
repeating for your view.
I love the dance I have with you.
I know your hand upon my waist.
How free I fly in your embrace.
A single dance is not as true
as the chance I have
to dance this life
with you.

"You're Going to See What Kind of Husband I Am"

At the wedding reception, my family members roasted me, telling stories of childhood chicanery. My brother, Paul, told how I used to make him run around the church next door to our house in his socks in winter three times before I allowed him to come back inside. When he later asked, "How was your honeymoon?' Frank said, "She made me run around the hotel in my socks three times before she would let me back into the room."

The truth about our honeymoon is that it was practically non-existent. The one thing I learned about Frank pretty early on was that he was not much of a planner. He had invited his family to our wedding, but had made it sound like no big deal, so no one came. He just wanted to "get it over with." For our honeymoon, he said we could just stop at a hotel on the way back to New York City. Frank had yet to move out of his apartment in Harlem, so we needed to use what little time we had to transport his belongings to our first home, a one-bedroom apartment in Borough Park, Brooklyn. When we got to Harlem the day after our wedding, I thought we were there to carry boxes to the car. Wrong. Nothing was packed but the apartment itself! Frank ended up inviting his friends over to take whatever they wanted off our hands.

Our apartment hunting was an eye-opening and painful experience. When the basement apartment in the building where I lived with Naomi became available, I asked my landlord if I could live there with Frank after we got married. He told me "no." He explained that it wasn't him; it was his brother. They were in the real estate business together and his brother would not be happy if he rented to a black man. I was shocked.

When Frank asked me, "What happened to the basement apartment?" I told him the ceilings were too low, which was true. Frank was tall, but he was also no fool. He just said, "Uh huh." I didn't have the courage to tell him what he already knew. He'd met my landlord a few times, and even helped shovel his driveway after a snowstorm, but that wasn't enough to break the twisted, hidden barrier that has caused so much grief.

I soon learned that he wasn't the only landlord in Brooklyn who thought this way. One after another, the apartments we could afford were closed to us once Frank walked through the door. I decided to go apartment hunting by myself. Frank sternly warned me, "You make sure you tell them I'm black. If they don't want you there, believe me, you don't want to be there." We talked about living in a black neighborhood, but Frank decided it would be better for him to deal with prejudice than have to worry about what I might have to deal with while he was away at work.

We finally found an affordable, one bedroom apartment in a Hasidic Jewish neighborhood. On that particular block there were just a few non-Jewish families, one of which owned a four-family house. The older couple who owned the house would not agree to rent to me until they met my soon-to-be husband. When I very hesitantly told them he was black, they were completely silent. Then, the husband, Franco, stood up and made the pronouncement: "You got the apartment because you're honest."

Of course, they still had to meet Frank, who was able to make an instant connection with our new landlord. One day Franco told me, "I like your husband *more* than you." And he wasn't the only one. Frank became a favorite in the neighborhood, especially on the Jewish Sabbath when the Jews were not permitted to do any work at all: this included turning lights on and off, using the stove and dialing the telephone. Frank was the neighborhood "Shabbat goy." On a Saturday morning he would emerge from a neighbor's apartment with a candy bar or a can of beer, a gift for his services.

Before we were married, Frank had told me, "You're going to see what kind of husband I am." He did not disappoint me. He was very helpful around the house, and quick to run errands. He enjoyed cooking and always cleaned up after himself. He even taught me a few tricks about folding clothes and ironing. He took pride in the little things he could do to help out. He also set up a work space for me with a computer, printer and fax machine, and did all the necessary upgrades and repairs. He was a devoted and doting husband who always told me that he loved me and would add, "I have the best wife in the world."

While we both agreed that married life was better than we thought it would be, there were still some bumps in the road. One day, we were having some sort of argument in the car. Frank pulled over by the hydrant outside our apartment. I got angry and got out of the car. Frank quickly got out and looked at me very seriously. "Rita, calm down.

Get in the car." I ran into the house instead. He came in about forty-five minutes later. I was wondering what had taken him so long, but since we were fighting, I figured he just needed some time to cool off. No. He was being interrogated by the police! They didn't believe that he lived in the neighborhood. They thought he was harassing me. He had had to prove to them that I was his wife and that he lived there.

Another difficulty we had to face was our different view of how our life together should look. I had imagined settling down and having children. Frank wanted to travel. During our marriage preparation with Albacete, Frank learned that to get married in the Catholic Church, he would have to agree "to accept children lovingly from God." Although he said he would, he was apprehensive about it. I told him that, due to my age, he may be worrying about nothing, and, after some discussion, we agreed to accept whatever the Lord had in mind for us as a couple, not taking any measures to avoid conception or to help it along, though I secretly hoped and prayed for fertility. Two months after my 40th birthday, my prayers were answered. I was overwhelmed with joy, and Frank was very nervous. He spoke to a woman at his job and she told him, "How can you be against your wife having a baby?" Her words struck a chord, and he softened. When we found out that the baby was a boy, Frank's acceptance turned to over the moon excitement. He ran through the halls at his job yelling, "It's a boy! My wife is having a baby boy!" Again, Frank was convicted. He remembered the promise he had made to Ben, whose little boy had passed away two years earlier: "If I ever have another son, I'm going to name him Micah."

As the baby grew inside, Frank and I grew as a couple. As soon as I discovered that I was pregnant, I called my psychiatrist. I had been on antidepressants for three years and was concerned about their effect on the baby. My doctor told me that there was no evidence that the medication could harm my child, but just to be on the safe side, I should see if I could slowly wean myself off. Of course, I stopped immediately, which caused me to smash a few things in the house, including Frank's carefully concocted "lotion potion," a bottle of mixed oils and skin moisturizers for his dry skin, that he had placed in front of the alarm clock, so I couldn't see what time it was. He told me, "The next time you break something of mine, I'm not going to say a word; I'm just going to go and break something of yours." I could think of a few precious items that I wanted intact; I gained amazing restraint.

But I wasn't the only one who had to learn impulse control. After just a few months of marriage, I was overwhelmed by all the "backup" items we had accumulated. My philosophy had always been, let the stores store; I'll buy when I need. Frank was the opposite. One day I realized we owned an elaborate collection of flashlights of various colors, shapes, sizes and intensities, each with its corresponding batteries, plus "backup" batteries. During the Northeast blackout of 2003, Frank had to walk home from his job in Manhattan. The first thing he said after he threw his "cheap Payless shoes" in the garbage was, "You see, these flashlights really come in handy." He even had one on his keychain, which he had used during the blackout to help strangers who'd lost their way on the dark street.

The flashlight discussion helped to shed light on the bigger issue: why we had very little money in our bank account. Frank did all the banking and paid the bills, so I hadn't paid much attention to our spending until we had a child on the way. I told Frank that it was inexcusable to have no savings when we were both working full time. I quickly drew up a budget, giving each of us more than adequate pocket money every month. But we hadn't even been using the new budget for a week when Frank sat me down and told me that we had to have a serious talk.

"I can't do this," he said.

"You have to."

"Please, give me the chance to prove to you that I can save money."

"No."

"I promise you that if I overspend, I will give you full control of the finances. Just give me one month to prove myself."

And Frank once again showed me that he was a man of his word. We saved ten thousand dollars in eight months!

Another obstacle we had to overcome was getting Frank a driver's license. The first step was going to the Department of Motor Vehicles in Hauppauge, Long Island to get copies of all of his outstanding tickets. He had fifteen years' worth of violations dating back to 1982—speeding tickets, tickets for driving without insurance, failures to answer summons, failures to pay fines, administrative adjudications, suspensions and revocations. He had so many violations that it took the clerk ten minutes just to print them out! Frank was telling jokes and had all the clerks and the people waiting in line laughing hysterically. One man told him, "You should be a comedian. You could make a lot of money!" Humor was Frank's way of coping with extreme stress. The more stressful the situation, the funnier the jokes.

Several court dates were set up, though most of the police officers who had written the tickets were retired or deceased. Nevertheless, he had to make all the court dates. Fortunately, our friend, Joe Wiener, was a lawyer, and his assistance made things much easier. Frank's brother-in-law, Alfred Townes, and our friend, Oleg Bredikhin also helped by driving him to Long Island for his court appearances. Once again, Frank found himself begging for mercy before a judge's bench, but this time he encountered very little sympathy. "Why should I reward you for such abuse of your privilege to drive?" Frank was humble in admitting his errors, but extremely persistent. When all the violations were settled or dismissed, and the penalties paid, Frank studied for his permit test. He took the little booklet on the subway and studied on his way to and from work. He passed with a perfect score. But the road test was a different story. Though Frank was a capable and confident driver, with quick reflexes and good depth perception, none of this counted when he failed to stop behind the demarcation line at a stop sign. Though he was shocked and disheartened, he immediately scheduled another road test. He had learned his lesson about stop signs, but the second time, he seemed to be unschooled when it came to the proper use of the right mirror. The road test examiner lectured him for several tense minutes before he gave him the news—he had passed!

We finally took a real honeymoon to Puerto Vallarta, Mexico, where his niece and childhood roommate, Dana (who really had become a medical doctor, as the family had predicted) offered us her timeshare as a wedding gift. I'm sure I would've had a great time were it not for the constant, first-trimester nausea. Frank took a lot of photos, and in every one I'm grimacing from morning sickness, which lasted all day!

The resort was very upscale. When people saw Frank walking around, they thought he was the famous Major League Baseball player, Darrel Strawberry. He was invited to several timeshare meetings. One place offered him a free jeep rental, just for attending. We drove it up a steep mountain road and had dinner at a restaurant at the top. That's where I learned that Frank had a fear of heights. He was anxious the entire time. When we drove back down, the jeep's clutch came off in Frank's hand! Fortunately his survival driving skills steered us to safety. His colorblindness was also an issue. In Mexico, the stop light colors were not as well differentiated as in the United States. I had to tell Frank what color the lights were.

The hotel had a magnificent swimming pool, but I needed to buy a new bathing suit, since, due to the pregnancy, I no longer fit into the top of my old one. We went to a department store, but I couldn't find anything that fit, so I decided to buy two bathing suit tops and rig them together in such a way that I had support from one and adequate coverage from the other. When we got back to the hotel and dressed for the pool, Frank looked at me and said,

"I am not going to be seen in public with you dressed like that."

I was shocked. That was the first (and last) time Frank ever complained about the way I was dressed. "What's wrong?" I asked. "Is it too immodest?"

"No!" He said. "You look like you're ashamed of your body."

We somehow reached a compromise, and were pleased to be able to swim outdoors in February, though the water was a bit chilly. Frank got a kick out of ordering exotic drinks by the poolside, and saying to the waiter, "Charge it to room 239."

When we returned from Mexico, Fr. Peter Cameron asked us if we would like to audition for a new play he had written, *The Drama of Light,* a series of skits about the luminous mysteries of the rosary. I was very surprised that he mentioned Frank, who had no acting experience, and even more surprised that Frank agreed to try out. We were both cast as members of the moving chorus. I discovered that Frank was excellent at singing harmony, and very diligent about memorizing his lines. Long after the play was over, he still remembered them, and would often walk around our apartment throwing them out whenever he deemed appropriate.

One of his favorites was a line used to highlight how human beings excuse their own lack of virtue by declaring, "That's just the way I am." That became Frank's first response every time I criticized him for doing something I didn't like, and he always said it emphatically, exactly as he had done in the play, which usually made me laugh, diffusing the entire situation. When I complained to him about the behavior of others, he would say, "impurity, sorcery, hostilities, jealousy, quarrels, rage, rivalries, dissensions, factions, drunkenness, and the like," which also made me laugh, taking the focus off whatever the offending behavior was.

That May, Frank's daughter, Wendi, was graduating from East Tennessee State University, and Frank really wanted to be there for her. We picked up Marshall and Frank's granddaughter, Daezhana, who was now five years old, in the car, and headed south. It was a long drive, but it was exciting to be traveling together as a family, and even more exciting to be celebrating Wendi's achievement. We stayed at her apartment, which was spacious and modern. At the graduation ceremony, Frank had a camera in one hand and a video camera in the other. Afterwards, we all went out to lunch at Ruby Tuesdays with Wendi's grandmother, Nan, who told us over and over again how happy she was that we were there for her granddaughter.

Not long after our trip, Marshall and Tanya split up, and Daezhana went to live in Oklahoma with her mother and maternal grandmother. Frank and I were filled with sorrow. Though I was pregnant and our family was growing, it also seemed to be growing apart.

I also learned that I had gestational diabetes. My OB/GYN sent me to a high-risk pregnancy doctor and a dietician. I had to check my blood sugar twice a day. I hate the sight of blood, but Frank was good with such things. He quickly took charge of pricking my finger and dripping the blood on the test strip, carefully monitoring my condition. He discovered that my sugar was never high unless I ate French fries.

"I Just Got Real Deep with God"

I was working as Assistant Director of English as a Second Language Programs at Kingsborough Community College, and was ready for a long weekend, as Labor Day was that Monday. Little did I know, Sunday would be *my* labor day. On Saturday night, I awoke from sleep and noticed my nightgown was damp, but I didn't make much of it because it was a hot night. Frank wanted to call the doctor in the morning, just in case. When the doctor told me that my water had broken, I was in disbelief. Where was the big splash? He told us to come in immediately. I was induced, but not much was happening except Hurricane Frances, which Frank was watching on TV as it battered the Florida coast. Frank loved storm stories, but little did we know that a new one was about to begin. The doctor entered the room and announced that I needed a C-Section. I started to cry. I was taken to another room where the anesthesiologist sat me on a table and told me not to move; he had to put a needle in my spine. The nurse, a small and serious West Indian woman, warned me that if I moved, I could become paralyzed.

"Help me, Jesus!" I cried out.

"Yes, Jesus!" the nurse said.

The epidural was a success, and Frank went to get dressed in scrubs and waited outside the operating room as the medical staff prepared me for surgery. When Frank came in, he was wearing a mask on his face, and his eyes were holding back tears. He seemed to have a desperate need to talk. He stood at the head of the bed, leaned down, and whispered through the mask into my ear, "I just got real deep with God."

"Me too," I said, becoming more and more terrified by the minute. I looked into Frank's eyes. He was trying to communicate something to me, something more than fear, but I couldn't understand what. His expression quickly changed when the doctors started to work. He became immensely curious and stood up to see over the blue sheet that sectioned off my bottom half from view.

"What's going on?" I had started to feel pressure.

"You're doing good," he said, but his attention had shifted from my face to the other side of the blue sheet. Throughout the procedure, he smiled to comfort me, and stroked my head, but kept looking intently over the blue sheet.

Within ten minutes, Micah came forth. He was perfect.

It was September 5th, the same day that my older brother, Bill was born, which meant that my mother's firstborn and my firstborn shared the same birthday.

Frank called Elvira Parravicini, a neonatologist and very close friend, whom I had lived with for the five years I had spent with the *Memores Domini*. She came immediately and reported that Micah was very strong and healthy, not to mention, she added, absolutely beautiful. The nurse came in and showed Frank how to change the baby, and clean around his navel, which still held part of the umbilical cord. Frank wanted to feed Micah, too, though I was trying to breastfeed. He took a lot of pictures and videos, and held Micah and kissed him continually. When visitors came, he made sure they were photographed holding his newborn son.

I later asked Frank about his pre-delivery prayer. He told me that he had never prayed so fervently, from the depths of his soul. "I begged God not to hold my past sins against my wife and child. It was deep," he said. Then he asked, "but how do you get to that level with God without having to suffer so much?"

For the next few days, Frank was in a constant state of euphoria. "I'm so excited, I can't even sleep!"

When I told him that he should try to get some rest after work instead of coming to the hospital, he became angry. "Why are you trying to keep me from my son?"

I was taken aback by Frank's response and later came to understand how deep the wounds were that he carried for all the years he was absent from the lives of his two older children. Micah's birth was bringing these wounds to the surface so the healing could begin. And, as it turned out, Micah's birth was able to heal some of my old wounds, too.

In 1985, I had entered the Missionaries of Charity as an Aspirant, that is, someone who wants to become one of the sisters. I remember seeing a preview of the movie "Mother Teresa," by Ann and Jeanette Petrie (whom I actually met when I lived in the main house in the Bronx). A line from the movie, spoken by Mother Teresa, has never left me: "The person whom Christ has chosen for Himself--she knows. Maybe she doesn't know how to express it, but she knows." I had always thought I "knew" I was that person.

One day when I was a Postulant (I had been with the sisters for over a year), my morning assignment was to clean the men's shelter "Queen of Peace." I was told by my mistress, Sister N, that there was an alcoholic man, who was very sick and couldn't leave the shelter. He was resting on the 4th floor, she said, and I must go up there and clean, but I was sternly warned not to talk to him. Fr. Brian Kolodiejchuk, MC was working to help the man, and had asked special permission for him not to have to leave the shelter during the day. So I went upstairs to do my usual cleaning, and there he was: tall, very thin, and desperately wanting to chat. He was following me around as I was disinfecting beds, and he asked me, "Why won't you talk to me?" He finally got me to crack a smile. I was embarrassed, but, at the same time, I felt very uncomfortable ignoring him. I tried to obey my instructions, but it seemed impossible. He was relentless for my attention. I did talk to him a bit, or maybe just listened, I don't remember, but afterwards, I felt so guilty that I went to Sr. N and confessed my fault.

Right around that time, Mother Teresa was visiting, and we had to turn in our letters requesting to move on to the Novitiate in San Francisco. That was a big move! Sr. N had never liked me. She went to Mother and told her that I was talking to the homeless man in the shelter. I felt so ashamed, like I had broken a marital vow. And when I went to talk with Mother Teresa, she was angry with me. She said, "Why were you talking to that man in the shelter? Be straight with me." I was very confused and deeply ashamed. I didn't know how to defend myself or even if I should. We were taught not to defend ourselves against accusations in order to be more like Jesus. So I think I said something like, "I don't know, Mother. I'm sorry." I wondered if I had developed inappropriate feelings for this homeless man.

Well, it wasn't long after that that my request to go to the Novitiate was rejected. I was given "6 more months" as a postulant "to deepen my love for Jesus." I was very upset because my best friend, Sr. Anthony, would be leaving me. We were forbidden from having "special friendships" as a way of being detached, so I shouldn't even have felt pain at the thought of separation. But how would I survive without her? Not only that, but I had to remain with Sr. N, who I was certain had no use for me. She made me do extra chores and berated me constantly. I felt she was trying to break me.

One day, I was sitting in the chapel, crying and shaking uncontrollably. I thought for sure that I was damned to hell and there was no way out. At the time there were many professed sisters visiting for a retreat in the house, and I was asked to make lunch. I was alone and had no one to consult about cooking the rice. The Indian sisters made it differently from the way I was taught, and they tried to impose their way on me, which never worked, but I was worried about disobeying, so I tried it their way. It was ten minutes before the *Angelus*, and I had made a mess of lunch. One American sister came downstairs and took pity on me. She told me not to worry, and gave me a can of tomatoes to open. When I punctured the can, red sauce came spurting out all over my white sari. I ran upstairs to the bathroom and locked myself in and didn't come out until after lunch.

Within the next day or two, Sr. Frederick, the regional superior, called me into her office and asked me what I wanted to do. That morning it had snowed for the first time, and I watched the children out the chapel window, catching snowflakes on their tongues and jumping joyfully in the snow. I want to be free, like them, I thought. So I told Sr. Frederick, "I think I want to leave." She said, "I think so, too." The next thing I knew, I was dressed in a skirt and blouse that had been donated to the shelter, and was heading to Newark Airport with Sr. N. We ended up going to the wrong terminal. I had my ticket in hand and I raced on foot to the next terminal without looking back. My life with the Missionaries of Charity had come to a flying end.

Even after my marriage to Frank, it was always very difficult for me to think about that chapter of my life without feeling intense shame. But when Micah was six months old, that all changed. I was performing in a passion play during Lent of 2005. Our theatre company traveled to Washington, DC to the Basilica of the Immaculate Conception, to perform the play in its crypt. During our dress rehearsal, out of the corner of my eye, I saw a small group of women dressed in the unmistakable white, blue-bordered sari of the Missionaries of Charity. The sisters were paying a visit to one of the side altars. I felt like I wanted to hide, although surely they would not recognize me. It had been almost twenty years since I had left, and besides, I was disguised as a Hebrew woman from the time of Jesus, wearing a floor length tunic and a head scarf. When I exited the performance space, I drew closer to the sisters to see if I could recognize any of them. Sure enough, Sr. Dominga was among them. She knew me very well. We had lived together for over a year. She was British and had a tremendous sense of humor.

I approached the group. "Hi, Sr. Dominga! Do you remember me? I was Sr. Janice."

"Of course!" she said, her bright blue eyes looking at me with delight. "Rita…right?"

"Yes! I don't usually dress like this, but I'm in a theater company and we're performing a passion play."

I expected her to crack a joke, but she simply said, "How are you?"

"I'm doing very well, Sister. I'm married and have a baby boy."

Her response surprised me: "What day was he born?"

"September 5th."

"That's Mother's feast day," she said, as if she'd known before she asked.

My feeling of utter amazement lasted about ten seconds, and then I felt terrible shame. I should've known the day Mother died. How could I have been so unaware? Maybe I needed to hear it from a Missionary of Charity, one who knew me, who knew my struggles and my history, so that there could be no doubt that Mother Teresa had had a hand in Micah's existence, the same way that Frank was convinced of his mother's prayers when he found himself in the hospital where she used to work after being rescued from a suicide attempt. Yes, it was clear. Mother Teresa wanted me to know that she loved me. She wanted me to be happy. She did not want me to feel shame, and it was through her intercession, and the intercession of Micah McKnight, that my firstborn son had come to be!

"My Boy Can Go Anywhere I Go"

Micah was a treasure, and Frank was completely enamored of him. He always wanted Micah near him. He'd run out the door carrying Micah in his car seat.

"Where are you going?"

"Me and my boy are going for a ride!"

"But he's just a baby!"

"My boy can go anywhere I go."

He'd take him to Anthony's apartment for a visit. But as soon as Anthony complained about dirty diapers stinking up his garbage, Frank ceased the visits.

If I had to go out, Frank was always happy to stay home with the baby. I would come home and find Micah sound asleep on the couch next to Frank.

"Why didn't you put him in his crib?"

"He likes to rest next to his father."

One night Frank was watching the movie "The Grudge" with Micah asleep in his arms. There was a scene in the movie where the telephone rings, someone hangs up, and then the Grudge enters, making a slurping sound. Though Frank loved horror films, this one frightened him so much that he had to turn the TV off. No sooner had he done so than the phone rang. The person on the other end hung up. This was followed by a sucking noise. Frank was about to go out of his mind until he discovered that it was Micah, sucking on his tee shirt!

Micah's existence brought Frank much closer to his family. When Frank's oldest sister, Bernice, was in town visiting from the Virgin Islands, we were invited to her daughter, Gerda's house in New Jersey to celebrate Bernice's seventy-second birthday. Frank's brother Kenny, and Kenny's wife Carol, both deaf mutes, were there, and admired our newborn son. Bernice gave us so many baby gifts, we almost forgot it was *her* celebration until the cake was brought out. She sang a song of thanksgiving to God, gesturing to each one of us. When she finished, we all clapped and said, "Amen!" Frank thought it was funny. His siblings were raised Roman Catholic, but not all of them had remained so. Kenny was a Jehovah Witness, Althea, a Buddhist. But when the family got together, there was great respect and space for other beliefs, and this allowed for joyful common worship.

Being a new mother at the age of forty-one had its challenges. I was afraid that every little noise would wake the baby, so once, when a Mitzvah tank (a Winnebago playing very loud Eastern European folk music) came down the block, I nearly lost my mind. Frank immediately broke into a Russian squat-and-kick move and kept dancing until I had no choice but to laugh. I was almost sad when the music stopped.

On Mother's Day, we made a trip out to Pinelawn Cemetery on Long Island with Frank's sisters, Emma and Althea, to visit their mother's grave. Christalia was born on May 4, 1915, and so it was particularly meaningful that she be remembered in the month of May. Although there was an extra plot, Frank's father was not buried there because he had remarried, and his second wife, Veronica, had had him cremated and his ashes placed in a columbarium at a Lutheran church near their home. When we left the cemetery, after placing flowers and saying prayers, Frank decided that he wanted to go to Amityville to wish Veronica a Happy Mother's Day. We all went together. When we got to her house, Emma and Althea refused to get out of the car. Frank took Micah in his arms, and I followed. He rang the bell, and a handsome black man who looked to be in his thirties answered the door. He was Veronica's son. Frank held Micah up and said, "It's me, Frank. I've come to wish your mother a Happy Mother's Day."

The man looked frightened. He disappeared and Veronica came to the door. She looked at Frank as if she were seeing a ghost. She opened the storm door very slowly and let us in. We walked into the kitchen and stood. Frank did most of the talking.

"I wanted to wish you a Happy Mother's Day. As you can see, I'm doing well." He introduced me and Micah.

I asked if I could have some water to put in Micah's bottle. Veronica didn't seem to hear me, so I asked again. "Oh, yes," she said, and told me to use the sink. We remained standing in the kitchen.

"Well, I didn't come to bother you," Frank said. "I just wanted you to see that my life is good, God has really blessed me, and I hope, since it's Mother's Day, we can leave the past behind us."

"Ok, well, thanks for coming," Veronica said, still stunned.

We said goodbye and drove off. "I really needed to do that," Frank said. His relationship with his stepmother was not a good one. Frank was deeply hurt by the way she treated him after his mother died. He was so angry with her that once, by his own admission, he had tried to run her over with a car. But marriage and family had changed Frank's heart. He wanted to be at peace with everyone, and he wanted Veronica to see that life had given him another chance.

Now that we had Micah, we had to revisit our openness to children. Frank was apprehensive about having more. He was almost fifty years old, and already a grandfather, and he did not see himself having another child. We agreed on a compromise. We would enroll in the Natural Family Planning course that we had neglected to take during our marriage preparation, as a way to prevent conception. Frank felt he was being very open by agreeing not to use artificial birth control, although it was sad for me, as one of ten children, because I knew the value of siblings and really wanted Micah to have a little brother or sister.

We enrolled in the only open course we could find. It was held in a church basement on Staten Island. When we entered the classroom, we realized we were the oldest and most earnest couple there. A portly older gentleman was the instructor. It was autumn, but he had the air conditioner on full blast. His wife, the co-instructor, was home sick, but she kept calling him on his cell phone, reminding him of this or that point that he needed to make. I was so cold, but I couldn't reach the air conditioner to turn it off, so I asked Frank to do it. Frank felt it wasn't his business, but I shivered and pestered him until he finally got up and shut it off. The instructor began sweating profusely. "Did someone turn the AC off?" he asked.

Frank sighed and raised his hand. "Your wife keeps calling you on the phone, but mine is sitting right here next to me."

Frank turned the AC back on and the instructor continued, but the quality of the instruction did not improve, and our attempts to ask questions about breastfeeding only seemed to mire the issue further in confusion. Needless to say, when we left, we weren't very confident in our knowledge of the natural method.

"No Son of Mine Is Going to Be Dressed like That!"

In June of 2005, I wanted to throw a big surprise party for Frank's 50th birthday. I invited his daughter, Wendi, who flew in from Tennessee. His son, Marshall, and his son's mother, Bobby Ann, came, plus Emma and her husband, Alfred and Althea. I also invited his friend, Anthony, and many of my family members, together with our mutual friends from the CL community. The party was held in the home of one of my former students, Julio Jimenez, and his wife, Miguelina. I really wanted to celebrate, but for some reason the wine tasted sour. Marshall and Wendi spent that night at our apartment, and, in the morning, Frank went out to buy some donuts. I took a bite of one. "Don't eat them," I said, "there's something wrong with them."

"They taste fine to me," Wendi said, and Marshall and Frank agreed.

I decided to take a pregnancy test. Sure enough, it came out positive. I was very happy, but also worried about how Frank would take the news. Within a week, I was vomiting, and I had to take care of a nine-month-old. Frank was going to find out sooner or later, so I decided to just tell him. When he got in from work, I gave him the news.

"You're happy about this," he said.

"Yes," I said, hoping he would smile.

He told me he needed to go for a walk. I was nauseous and upset. I phoned Monsignor Albacete. He was very happy about the news, and told me not to worry; he would talk with Frank.

As the days went by, Frank adjusted to the idea of being the father of a fourth child. I had terrible morning sickness and vomited so often that the doctor prescribed Reglan, which kept me from throwing up, but did not take away the nausea. At the same time, my father's health was deteriorating, and I really wanted to spend time with my family upstate. Frank agreed that it would be good for me to get away, so I planned a trip to see my parents, and of course I would take Micah with me. Frank had previously threatened to get a vasectomy, and I was afraid he would do it in my absence. When I confronted him with my fears, he said, "You can't just go and have that done. You need to have counseling first."

I wasn't worried after that, first because Frank was a procrastinator, and second because, as my brother-in-law, Ken, later confirmed, "Frank respects you too much to do something you so strongly disapprove of."

I never fully understood Frank's objections to a second pregnancy, but I know that we never would have gotten through it without the help of Msgr. Albacete and Ken, whom Frank wanted to be our second child's godfather.

On November 2, 2005, All Soul's Day, the day the whole Church prays for the dead, my father, William Theodore Flansburg, breathed his last. I was fortunate to see him not long before he died. Knowing my father and I both had strong personalities, which often clashed, Frank encouraged me to say whatever I needed to say to him before he died, but when I saw him so thin and peaceful and accepting of his destiny, I found no reason to tell him anything except, "I love you, Daddy."

"Eternal Rest"

I always figured
we'd never got along.
My father was unyielding.
A man of his word,
aware of his duty's worth.
But right before he died,
his face was like a little boy's.
He hadn't the strength
to lift his lids
but when we prayed
he struggled to join in.
"In the Name of the Father,"
he heard us say
and almost touched his brow
in effort to obey.
How hard he tried
right to the end.
I never loved him more
than when we said "Amen."

Frank immediately asked for a couple days off from work, and we drove upstate to Lima, New York, for the funeral. There were so many people at the calling hours that the line extended out the door. Many of my friends and family members got to meet my husband for the first time. My mother was very, very sorrowful. She'd been married to my father for forty-five years and they had raised ten children together. But she told me that, in spite of her sadness, she was very happy about the new baby on the way. "New life," she said.

109

For Thanksgiving that year, we went back upstate to spend it with my mother, who for the first time, decided not to cook. Instead, we made dinner reservations at the same restaurant where Frank and I had had our wedding reception.

As soon as we got back to Brooklyn, with the new baby coming in just a couple months, we had to start preparing to move into our new apartment. This one had been even more difficult to find than the first one.

Back in summer, when I first found out I was pregnant, it was nearly impossible to motivate Frank to look for a new place. He would rather have squeezed us all into one bedroom than go through what we went through before, but I was unyielding. We had to start hunting, and we both knew it wouldn't be easy. Frank was the only one working, and though we had done well with our finances, rents were very high. And then, it was the same old story: we would find a place we could afford and, as soon as Frank appeared, the price went up, or the place was no longer available. I was starting to despair. I went to confession and told the priest that I had no faith.

The priest, instead of admonishing me, encouraged me. He promised to pray for me and my family. He was certain that I didn't have to worry.

In the meantime, my sister Naomi had married Ken Genuard. Ken's mother, Marie, was checking the apartment listings every day and calling me when she saw something that might work for us. I had a list of three places in our price range that she had seen advertised in the local Catholic newspaper. I made an appointment to look at them on Saturday, when Frank was home. He was becoming discouraged, too, and didn't want to go, but I was six months pregnant and not taking "no" for an answer. We went to see a nice-sized two-bedroom in a decent neighborhood, not too far from my two sisters, and in our price range. The landlord was fixing the place up. It was spacious, and had a new kitchen and bathroom. We liked it immediately. "We'll take it," Frank said.

"I'll let you know," the landlord said, "I've got other people who are coming to look at it."

My heart sank. He wasn't going to rent to us. He was an Italian American, and the neighborhood was full of St. Anthony statues. "I'm going to pray to St. Anthony!" I said, defiantly, and walked out the door.

I did say a prayer to St. Anthony, but I also decided to pray to Fr. Giussani, the founder of Communion and Liberation, who had passed away in 2005. After crying out to him, an idea popped into my head. We had resources. Ken's parents were Italians from Brooklyn. They could call the landlord and give us a recommendation.

I called Marie and told her we had seen an apartment that we really liked, but it didn't seem like the landlord wanted to rent to us. "Do you think you could call him and recommend us?"

Marie said she would ask her husband, John. John immediately called the landlord, Mario. John explained that his son had married my sister, and that if he weren't selling his house to move to New Jersey, he and his wife would've loved to rent to us. He said that Frank and I were both very hard-working, honest people. No sooner had Marie relayed the conversation to me than we got a call from Mario. "I've never gotten such a glowing recommendation. If you want the apartment, it's yours."

We drove over to Mario's house with one month's rent and one month's deposit, in cash. Mario invited us to come in and sit down. Frank gave him the money and told him that he wouldn't regret his decision. We moved in on January 1, 2006. On many occasions when Mario came to collect the rent, Frank would say to him, "We're good tenants, aren't we?" Mario always agreed, but Frank said it so often it embarrassed me.

Something I never would have anticipated was the difficulty Frank and I had agreeing on a name for our second child, especially because he had told me that, since he had named Micah, I could name this next baby. Months earlier, the ultrasound technician declared that the baby was "80% a girl." That didn't sound very scientific, but I went out and bought some pink outfits nonetheless. Frank and I fought furiously over the girl's name. When I told him I liked the name Maria, he said, "No." One name after the other he started shooting down, until we could only agree on one, Angelica, which was far from my favorite, but Frank agreed that her middle name could be Georgia, after my mother.

"What if it's a boy?" I said.

"I won't argue," he said.

"Okay, Martin Ambrose."

"Ambrose? No way! How about Martin Frank?"

I preferred Francis to Frank, and that was another debate which lasted some minutes. In the end, Frank's stubbornness, and his name, won out.

"Okay, Martin Frank if it's a boy, which, according to the technician, there's only a 20% chance," I said. And we actually shook on it, which I thought was even funnier.

I was scheduled to have a caesarian section on February 6, 2006, two weeks before the actual due date. After much deliberation, it was the safest way to go, considering I was 42 years old and had already had one C-Section. There was a snowstorm that day. My mother was in town, taking care of Micah while Frank was with me at the hospital. When I went to have the epidural, the anesthesiologist said, "You're going to have your tubes tied, right?"

"No!" I shouted, and started to get off the table.

"Please don't get her upset," Frank said, holding me back. "But you can tie mine."

"That makes me just as upset," I said.

Unlike my first delivery, once I had the epidural, nothing in the world could have disturbed me. I was joyful the whole time the doctor was cutting across my belly. When they pulled the baby out, the doctor said, "It's a boy!"

"How could you miss that?" Frank said, spotting the disproportionately large testicles on the 6-pound, 9 ounce baby.

"It's a boy!" I said, tears rolling down my face. Micah had a little brother, a beloved and life-long companion.

I had a drawer full of pink clothes for our newborn son. "There's no way he's going to wear those," Frank said, and went out in the blizzard to buy some boy outfits. He came back with some pinstriped pajamas in honor of his favorite baseball team, the Yankees.

Frank fought so hard for that middle name, and it was fitting. Martin looked a lot like Frank, and very early on started exhibiting many of his father's traits. He had Frank's sense of adventure and mischievousness, and was always on the move. He was also very forthright with his affections and displeasures, so different from his brother's calm and agreeable character. Micah could amuse himself for hours with little toys and books. He slept through the night and never fought me at nap time. I remember coaching young mothers, thinking that Micah's disposition was all due to my parenting skills. When Martin came along, I had to eat humble pie. If Martin didn't like something, you knew it immediately. My neighbor, Giovanna, used to yell in my window, "Rita, the baby's crying!" Such was the power of Martin's outbursts if you put him down for one minute to attend to anything else. He was so active that, for years, I had to strap him into his high chair just to get him to sit still and eat! When I dropped Micah off at his pre-K class, Martin would run into the classroom and not want to leave. When I brought him back home, he would be so angry that he would refuse to go into the house. Once I called Frank at work, completely frustrated. "He's three years old. You can't let him overpower you like that." Frank was very firm with Martin. "He's just like me," he would say. "You can't let him get away with things."

"God Is Getting Ready to Ask Something Really Big of Me"

Though our hands were full with the two boys, so was our life as a family. Frank's presence on weekends and after work made a big difference. We loved to take trips to Coney Island and put the boys on the kiddie rides or stroll them along the boardwalk in their double stroller. After Mass on Sunday, we took them to brunch with other families in our CL community, or to the playground where we pushed them on the swings or caught them at the end of the slide. During the week, when Frank came home from work, the first thing he did was drop his bags at the top of the stairs, and chase the boys around the dining room table. He bathed them, and changed them, and took them for haircuts, and sometimes even cut their hair himself. He would often say, in a high-pitched voice, "my little boys."

When I had to go out for the evening, Frank had no trouble staying at home and watching them. They loved to watch cartoons together. Eventually Frank knew all the words to the *Little Einstein* and *Barney* videos. He would go around the house singing the Hebrew alphabet, which he learned from watching *Barney in Concert*. Frank baked the boys corn bread, which Martin says was the best he ever tasted.

Once Micah had an accident on the dining room rug, and before Frank could clean it up, Martin went running right through it. When I got home, the kids were sound asleep, and Frank relayed the story to me like it was a great adventure. I was concerned about excrement all over my rug until he explained, in detail, all the steps he took, and the various chemicals he used to clean it up. "Besides," Frank said, "I'm not afraid of a little do-do. When I worked with the developmentally disabled, they used to reach right in the bowl and throw it at me."

Naptime was nonnegotiable. As older parents, we needed the rest as much as the kids did. On the weekends, the whole family was asleep after lunch. Even on vacation, we didn't sacrifice naptime. My brother Bill called us "the sleeping family."

On Halloween, Frank enjoyed carving pumpkins with the boys. He designed such peculiar faces that Micah laughed and Martin cried.

One day we went to visit an elderly priest who was a dear friend, Fr. Richard Nielson. He was retired and lived on Cape Cod with his friend, Donald. When we arrived at the house, after a long drive, the boys started running around and knocking things over. I was trying very hard to maintain control, but it was useless. There were fragile knickknacks everywhere! Donald was very upset by the ruckus. We had to cut the visit short. I was humiliated by my children's behavior, and amazed by Frank's calm. As we were driving away I asked him, "Aren't you embarrassed by the way the boys tore up their house?"

"I am never going to be ashamed of my children," he said, "because they're a gift."

After Cape Cod, we drove to the CL Family Vacation in New Hampshire. We spent five days hiking, swimming, singing, and gathering for prayer and discussion in the beautiful New Hampshire countryside. I was feeling the desire to participate more and more in the life of the community, and I desperately wanted Frank to be a part of it. One way to do this, which CL encourages, is to form a small group of close friends, called a small fraternity group, who help one another to live life intentionally and accompany one another through life's ups and downs. After the vacation, I asked some friends if they would form a small fraternity group with me, even though many of them, Frank included, had not taken formal steps to be members of Communion and Liberation. Those who accepted were George and Stacy Lugo, Luca Grillo, Tiffiny Gulla, Julio and Miguelina Jimenez, John and Flor Hendricksen, Fr. Anthony Bature, Tom Sullivan and Lupe Diaz. We met once a month, often at our house.

Frank wasn't much for formality, but he greatly enjoyed close personal relationships with people. George Lugo was a Yankee fan, so the two of them often got together and watched baseball. Julio and Fr. Bature would consult Frank about his knowledge of computers and other technical things. I would try and push the more formal aspect of the fraternity, but Frank didn't like anything that was too organized, though he very much enjoyed the dinners and discussions we would have.

One week my boys and I got sick with norovirus. I spent two straight days taking care of sick children, and then I got sick. Since Frank was at work, I called my sisters and they came over and helped disinfect the house and care for the boys while I lay in bed. Susan put them down for a nap and left, but Martin climbed out of his bed, got ahold of a black permanent marker, and wrote all over the furniture, walls and computer. I heard him moving around, but was too sick to get out of bed. When Frank came home, the kids were out of control and the house was a mess. Frank got very angry and spanked Martin and put both boys in bed, then he took rubbing alcohol and cleaned the black scribble that was everywhere.

In a day or two, I started feeling better physically, but I was emotionally devastated from the experience. I no longer desired to do anything that I didn't have to do, and I realized that, through my desire to involve Frank in the community, I had taken on too many responsibilities, including our small fraternity. I felt like, if I stopped caring about getting together, the group would fold. I waited a month to see if anyone else would ask about meeting, and when no one even called to inquire, I told everyone that I quit. Frank told me that I was making a mistake, but he didn't want the organizational responsibility either, and it seemed no one else was in a position to lead. So we no longer got together as a group, though we remained friends.

A growing desire for closeness with God led Frank to purchase an overpriced Bible on DVD. Frank was not a big fan of reading, so he felt that seeing the words on a large screen and hearing them read aloud would help him learn the Word of God. I was angry about the purchase because I knew that he would quickly lose interest. He told me I was wrong, and went into the living room and loaded the first disc of the New Testament, the genealogy of Jesus in the Gospel of Matthew. The words droned on, "And Judas begat Phares and Zara of Thamar; and Phares begat Esrom; and Esrom begat Aram…" Frank was becoming impatient. "And Ezekias begat Manasses; and Manasses begat Amon; and Amon begat Josias…"

"This is ridiculous," Frank said. "I can't sit here and listen to this!" And he shut it off.

Fortunately, there were bonus DVDs with multiple choice questions on them, which he played with the boys, giving him some return on his investment.

Frank was excelling at his job and had made a lot of friends. One was a lawyer named Joni Walaski. She, like Frank, had a passion for the Yankees, and she couldn't always use her season tickets, so she would offer them to Frank. He was able to take many of his friends and our boys to see games. One day, Joni and Frank had a discussion which turned into an argument. Afterwards, she stopped speaking to Frank. He was deeply hurt, but, although he tried to make amends, for whatever reason, he was unable to mend the relationship.

Eventually, Frank began attending the weekly Communion and Liberation meeting, "School of Community," where we study the texts written by the founder, Luigi Giussani, and compare the words we read with our experience. Frank attended the meeting at St. Patrick's Church in Bay Ridge with, among others, my sisters, Susan and Naomi, and their husbands, Jonathan Fields and Ken Genuard.

"At first, I was really resistant," Frank said. "I kept asking, 'who is this Giussani guy, anyway?'" But then he began to notice that these people, and the books they read "described true things I had seen in my life." He was amazed by the depth of the friendships that developed. "Slowly, I began to look at myself differently, and this took me in another direction." Because our children were young and needed care, I attended a different school of community at Sacred Hearts and St. Stephen's Church in Carroll Gardens, Brooklyn.

Frank was always eager to share what he had learned in his group. "Truth speaks for itself," he would say. "You don't have to sell it. It touches places of desire in your heart, and it is up to you to respond or not." At each school of community, we discussed a passage taken from the writings of the founder of Luigi Giussani. Often I would read the text aloud to Frank, and he would listen intently, nodding his head when he got the point that he felt he needed to get. And once he got it, he would stop me and say, "Okay, that's enough."

When Ken first brought Frank to the meetings, Jonathan was the leader. He recalled, "We were all superficial, and Frank just chimed in and cut to the core of things […]. And he loved his freedom […] You couldn't force Frank. He had to experience it; it had to be true for him. And when it was true, he followed it and never veered from it." He noted how quickly Frank was changing. "He was growing by leaps and bounds…"

To Jonathan, Frank was "a man of reason." "Frank used to say to me all the time, 'Jon, you're complaining to me right now. That means you exist. […] Even your complaining is a sign of your existence.'" and Jonathan started to use that reasoning himself. Frank's "embrace, his tenderness, his strength helped me to learn what I could not learn before."

Jonathan was so impressed, that at once he pointed at Frank and predicted, "You're going to lead the community one day."

Frank's fast learning curve and charisma were becoming quickly apparent throughout the community at large. Christopher Bacich was the head of CL in the US at the time, and he asked Frank to give a witness about his conversion to the high school students in the community.

Soon Frank was traveling around the country, talking about his experience.

It wasn't long before Frank was leading the school of community. If a friend didn't show up for a couple weeks, he would call him or her on the phone. He never pressured anyone, but just spoke from his heart about his desire to be with those he loved. Jonathan would later say, "Everyone could love Frank because Frank loved everyone's freedom."

Sometimes no one showed up for the meeting. In that case, Frank would sit in the room anyway and read the text. "I go to the School of Community because it is an invitation from Christ," he said.

During this time, Jonathan was struggling greatly. "I was learning two new jobs, and was constantly overwhelmed by my mistakes and limitations, losing my faith, becoming cynical, angry, insecure, and distancing myself from my wife and kids." Jonathan observed how calm and patient Frank was with everyone, particularly Susan, Jonathan's wife. "It was tough because I went to the meetings with my wife and I became impatient with her in front of everyone. But Frank was so calm and he would listen to her with great patience, and calm me down. He let everyone speak the way they wanted to speak, and believed the truth came out in the personality of the other, exactly the way it came out. He befriended my wife, loved my children, and corrected me strongly to try to listen, and also to be grateful, even though I was going through difficult times."

When Jonathan and Susan's son, Peter, made his First Communion, Frank was right there with camera in hand. This caused Peter some anxiety because his teachers had sternly warned all the children that no pictures were allowed to be taken in the church. When Frank heard this, it was like an invitation to do exactly the opposite. And sure enough, when it came Peter's time to receive Communion, Frank moved right to the front of the church and snapped the photo. At the time, Peter was mortified, but he later reflected: "We think that in order to change the world, affect a lot of people, there's something really big we have to do, but Frank was just himself, and that was the only thing he ever gave to every single person he ever met."

One day in the Spring of 2009, Frank told me, "I feel like God is getting ready to ask something really big of me." He didn't know what, but he awaited another invitation. He soon got a call from our choir director, Chris Vath, who was also the main organizer of Communion and Liberation's annual Good Friday Way of the Cross procession over the Brooklyn Bridge. The tradition began in 1995 with just a handful of participants, but grew every year, and in the wake of 9/11, added a stop at Ground Zero. Chris wanted Frank to carry the cross at the head of the procession. Frank embraced the invitation with great seriousness and conviction. He later reflected, "It was a great privilege...I was proud. I used that moment to reflect, and I think for once in my life I was selfless. I prayed for everyone else except me. I prayed for everyone—even the people who don't believe in God or Christ. I asked Him to rain blessings on everyone. I said that if there was something left over, then bless me and my family."

During the walk, Frank heard someone shouting his name. It was his friend, Earl Nixon, the one who had shared his refrigerator box with him when he was homeless in East New York.

He said, "I'm proud of you, man. I'm proud of you!"

"Walk with me, man! Walk with me!" Frank shouted back.

Earl couldn't because he was on his way to class at Pace University, on the Manhattan side of the Brooklyn Bridge, but they got in touch again later. He, like Frank, had survived and rebuilt his life. "It touched me to my soul," Frank said, remembering the life they had shared on the streets compared to the life they were living now.

The next morning, Frank's picture appeared in the *Daily News* with an article by Tim Persinko entitled "He crosses a bridge – from bad to good."[3] The article begins:

A recovering drug addict with a lifetime of burdens carried a wooden cross at the head of a Good Friday procession of 3,000 New Yorkers across the Brooklyn Bridge Friday.

Frankie Simmonds bore the pine cross from St. James Cathedral in downtown Brooklyn to City Hall Park, silently offering prayers for himself and his loved ones.

"I was praying for strength as I was walking," said Simmonds, 54, of Gravesend. "I had a list in my pocket of friends that asked me to pray for them, I carried it next to my heart."

---

[3] Tim Persinko, "He crosses a bridge – from bad to good," *NY Daily News*, April 11, 2009. https://www.nydailynews.com/new-york/brooklyn/crosses-bridge-bad-good-article-1.363165

The Doorkeeper

Following the financial crisis of 2008, Frank's job underwent some changes. His boss, Bobby Tannenhauser, was leaving the company, and its future was uncertain. Frank knew that Bobby owned a building in Manhattan on West 72nd Street between Central Park West and Columbus Avenue, and he was looking for a doorman. Frank jumped at the opportunity. It was a union job with full benefits, and, best of all, Frank could continue to work for Bobby, whom he loved like a father.

His career as a doorman began on August 18, 2009. Frank worked the night shift, and would treat all the dogs to doggy biscuits when their owners passed by the desk to take them out for walks in the early morning hours. Mike, a homeless man, used to walk by the building and sell Frank items he had found in the street. Once Frank came home with two large Samurai swords. "Where did you get those?" I asked, in horror.

"Mike sold them to me."

Another man, Joe, gave Frank baseball cards to give to our children. At Christmastime, Frank received beautiful notes from the residents of the building, thanking him for his kind greeting and bright smile. He was well loved, and many people were very generous with their Christmas tips.

Sometimes I called Frank in the middle of the night when I happened to be awake. Once he answered the phone laughing and out of breath. "What's going on?" I asked.

"I'm chasing Raymond around with a broom." Raymond Melendez was Frank's friend who worked as a porter. They horsed around like little kids.

Though I was in my mid-40s, fertility was still an issue. Besides having our two boys, I had gotten pregnant four other times, each resulting in miscarriage. I was adamant about not practicing artificial birth control, but our introduction to natural methods had been anything but clear. Naomi told me that there was a woman in Brooklyn who taught an advanced form of Natural Family Planning called the Creighton Model. This method was more scientific and effective in predicting a woman's fertility. I told Frank that I wanted us to take classes. He said that I could go, but he refused. I begged him to participate. He came to the first lesson, and that was it.

I began charting my cycle with great diligence, but the whole thing was less than appealing for Frank, and seemed to leave him cold. I soon discovered that he was chatting with old girlfriends online and felt completely betrayed. He was angry with me for invading his privacy and felt that his conversations with other women were harmless. "You don't get it; I'm just talking mess," he would say. Our differences were coming to a head. We needed help. I asked my brother-in-law Ken if he would speak to Frank and help him understand why I was so upset about his behavior. Ken agreed, and it helped a lot.

In November of 2009, we became godparents of Ken and Naomi's little girl, whom they adopted at birth and named Georgia Ann, after my mother. Frank also became a grandfather for the second time. Marshall had gotten married, and in March 2010, he and his wife, Camille, had a little boy, Matthew.

Frank continued to be asked each year to lead the Good Friday procession over the Brooklyn Bridge. The children were growing. Frank bought Micah a bicycle with training wheels, which were very quickly removed. When the boys started school, Frank attended every event with his camera and video camera fully charged. He cried when he saw the boys singing in the choir or dancing on the stage. They also were starting to play basketball and baseball in neighborhood leagues, and they took swimming lessons.

With both boys in school, I started attending a Wednesday morning School of Community at Saint Andrew's Church in Bay Ridge, Brooklyn. That's where I met an older woman, Angie Delillo. She was spunky and straightforward, and her life had been riddled with a lot of sorrow. She had lost her husband to cancer, and her son, Paul, was in a sledding accident when he was a teenager, which had left him paralyzed and in a wheelchair for the rest of his life. Paul lived with his mother, and when she became sick with lung cancer, Paul did not want visitors. This caused me a lot of pain. I had no sooner talked to Frank about it, then he immediately got on the phone and persuaded Paul to let me see his mother. We all knew she wasn't long for this world. Angie passed away soon after our visit.

Angie's an old friend.
I met her in her 70s.
She liked to tell me things
like why the birds
that perch on wires
don't crowd together
but give each other equal space
between their feathered frames.

127

Angie's son did not want guests
when his mother became sick.
I tried to see her, nonetheless.
Just in the nick of time.
She lay in bed and said my name.
"You're such a loyal friend;
You've been here every day."

She saw me when I wasn't there.
I see her just the same.

She visits in the empty space
between the perching birds—
the space they need to spread their wings
before they fly away.[4]

Frank was gaining confidence and becoming a leader. Before long, Jonathan's prophecy came true: Chris Bacich asked him to lead the New York CL community. Frank felt it was a great honor, and this new responsibility, as well as his growing friendship with my sister, Susan, caused him to become more and more curious about the CL Fraternity (the organization of all the adults in Communion and Liberation, officially recognized by the Catholic Church), and the purpose of the small fraternity group, and how it was different from the weekly School of Community meetings he was already attending. Susan began having conversations with him about it. She, too, was trying to understand, as her small fraternity group had also broken up. Frank did not speak with me about it, as I was not ready to embark on another failed group, but he continued having conversations with Susan, and eventually they decided to form their own group.

---

[4] Rita A. Simmonds, "Angie," *Well-Read Mom Newsletter*, 2017.

"Ok, I will be in a fraternity with you," he said, and started to call her "Suzy Wooz" and "my secret fraternity sister." Susan would later share their story:

If I had a problem or concern, he followed up. When I get stressed, I get insomnia. Frank worked nights. He told me, "Call me when that happens. You know I'm awake."

He commented on experiences we had together. Frank...had acrophobia but wanted to follow the gestures [at the CL summer vacation] and went on the big hike anyway. At the top of the mountain, he became very affected. I offered to walk back down with him. No big deal. We walked back down together, got to the bottom, looked up and waved to everyone at the top. Many, many times he commented to me about how much it meant to him to be accompanied.

He bought a new car and came to my house to show me. "I know this is not a big deal for most people," he said, "but when I think of where I came from, and where I am now, I'm real proud. I changed. I wanted to show you because it's more than the car."

I changed jobs. I started to work full-time. It was a very difficult job and in many ways went badly. I worked in the administration and was to become director of a soup kitchen and women's shelter, a place Frank knew well as, during his time on the streets, he had eaten there often. Getting through that job was a real New York story, a navigational nightmare. Frank was there with an insight I did not have. I have never been homeless. There were objective difficulties at this job, and injustices, terrible injustices. Frank was a rock. He was able to judge the situation. I just couldn't. With his companionship, with his clarity, I remained in a tough situation until I changed jobs.

From time to time, my sense of "formalism" crept in. I would ask Frank about inviting people into our group, and having meetings. Frank had this facial expression that communicated a mix between discomfort and irritation. "I don't feel obligated to do that," he'd say, "That's not what this is for me."

One year after I came home from the fraternity exercises (Frank could not go because of work), I called him and said, "You know, we need a prayer. Something simple. We just pray it every day for the intention of our fraternity."

"Ok, that's cool."

"Whatever you want; it can be the Our Father."

So it was the Our Father. It was his prayer of preference. He called me, almost daily, "Yo, Suzy Wooz, Let's do it!" Later, we would pray the Angelus.

In 2010, my mother's sister, Patricia Davis, was diagnosed with glioblastoma, an incurable brain cancer. We decided to meet my mother and brothers, Paul and Joe, at the Kateri National Shrine in Fonda, New York and pray for a miracle. Kateri Tekakwitha was born in that region in 1656, nine years after the first North American martyrs, the Jesuits Isaac Jogues and Jean de Lelande, were tomahawked to death by Iroquois in that region. Kateri converted to Christianity and suffered a great deal for it. At the time of our pilgrimage, she had not yet been canonized, but would be two years later. I was surprised at how willingly Frank went along with the whole pilgrimage idea. The prayers to Saint Kateri seemed to be working, as my aunt was living beyond what the doctors had expected.

In February of the following year, on the day before Martin's fifth birthday, I got a call from my sister, Regina, relaying yet another family tragedy. Our brother Paul was in a serious car accident and we didn't know if he was going to make it. I was driving when I got the news, and I tried to call Frank, who was home sleeping and didn't answer the phone. I didn't know what to do. I called my friend Tiffiny. She was in the car with her uncle. She asked him to pull over to the side of the road so she could say some serious prayers. When I got home, I ran upstairs and woke Frank up. I asked him if we should cancel Marty's birthday party which we were going to have that evening. He told me to wait and see. I called my mother. She told me, "You have that birthday party for that little boy!" It was decided. Family and friends came and, before the festivities, we gathered around our dining room table to pray the rosary. Frank was sitting at one end of the table, and Martin the other. Martin wanted to lead the prayer, and he did so with such strength and clarity that, when we finished, Frank proclaimed, "This is a birthday that Martin is never going to forget because he prayed for his Uncle Paul, and Paul's going to live."

Paul was T-boned by a young man who ran a red light, but walked away from the accident. Paul, on the other hand, had to be removed from his vehicle by the jaws of life and rushed to the hospital. He was operated on immediately. He had a torn aorta, shattered pelvis, broken ribs and brain bleeds. When I saw him, he was unconscious, and had all sorts of tubes hooked up to his body. Miraculously, he survived and was able to walk again, but was left disabled for the rest of his life.

After Paul's accident, I started to become fearful riding in the passenger's seat when Frank was behind the wheel. He drove too fast and took too many risks. This caused a growing tension between us whenever we got in the car together. Road trips, which used to be a source of great joy, became a cause for anxiety.

Our family began attending Regina Pacis Church in Dyker Heights, Brooklyn because my brother-in-law Jonathan was the music director there and had asked if our son Martin, who loved to sing, would join the children's choir. We sat in the front, near the choir. Frank was a great support to Jonathan: "One Sunday I was playing the keyboard a little too energetically, and it crashed to the floor. Frank came over and very quietly helped me pick up the piano, and kept looking at me so I would remain calm."

Regina Pacis is also where we met Deacon Ramon Pons, who was the same age as Frank and shared a similar history. He gave a very impassioned sermon about his conversion and the importance of the sacrament of reconciliation. Frank hadn't been to confession in forty years, arguing that he didn't need a priest as an intermediary; he could open his heart and confess his guilt to Christ directly. But the Deacon's sermon gave him something to think about. That Ash Wednesday, Frank was driving by the church and saw a big sign on the front: "CONFESSIONS ALL DAY." He went in and saw another sign, "Confessions Here" with an arrow pointing down at the pastor, Msgr. Ronald Marino, who was sitting right in front of him in a chair. Frank realized he was the first in line. The 40-year dry spell ended right there.

That summer, Frank began a new hepatitis C treatment. He again became very sick and lost a lot of weight, but the blood tests revealed that the treatment was working. On New Year's Day, 2012, we went to Mass at Regina Pacis. A badly shaken Deacon John Dolan delivered the homily and informed us that Deacon Ramon Pons had passed away the night before. He had been sick with liver cancer. This tragic news gave Frank the push he needed to persevere in his treatment, which he continued for three more months, until the virus had become undetectable. Frank was delighted, but also sick and weak. The doctor wanted him to continue the treatment, but Frank's body couldn't handle it. He stopped taking the medication. His strength returned, but, within three months, the virus did, too.

At that time, our friend, Fr. Rich Veras, organized a series of Lenten presentations at St. Rita's Church on Staten Island where he was pastor. One of the events was a talk on Saint Padre Pio given by another friend, Maria Teresa Landi, the daughter of Edgardo and Dina Landi, doctors who worked for Saint Pio in the Casa Sollievo della Sofferenza, the hospital he established in 1956 in San Giovanni Rotondo, in the Foggia province of Italy. Maria Teresa's parents had been married by Padre Pio. In her presentation, she related how, whenever he granted a miracle, a pleasant perfume filled the air. After Maria Teresa's talk, the attendees gathered in the back of the church for the unveiling of a new statue of Saint Pio, donated by some families of the parish. The "statue room" was noisy and crowded, so, immediately after the unveiling, I took the novena prayer card Fr. Rich had handed out, and went to pray before the Blessed Sacrament at the front of the church. I wanted to ask Padre Pio to heal Frank's hepatitis C. When I went to genuflect, I felt a terrible pain in my knee. It had been bothering me for months, but the cold church made it worse. I told Padre

Pio that I would accept that pain as a humiliation, if he could just heal Frank. I did a little curtsy before the Blessed Sacrament and read the novena prayer. When I had finished, I went to curtsy again, and noticed my knee didn't hurt! I went to genuflect again, and bent my knee all the way to the floor—no pain! I did it again. No pain! One more time—no pain! Padre Pio had healed my knee! I ran downstairs where people were having cookies and coffee and told everyone what had happened. Fr. Rich's secretary, Mary Grace Liss, was waving her finger in the air. It had miraculously straightened after years of being bent! I was so excited by the healings that I couldn't wait to see the miracle that Padre Pio would procure for Frank. When I got home, I ran to the top of the stairs and smelled a very strong vanilla scent. "Frank, Frank, do you smell that smell?" I said, bursting into our bedroom.

He was just getting to sleep, as he had to work later that night. "What's the matter with you?"

"Do you smell that smell?"

"Yes, I just went to the bathroom and sprayed some air freshener."

"But it's not air freshener," I said, still hopeful. "It's a very strong vanilla scent that I've never smelled before."

Frank became animated. "Yes, that's what someone at the job gave me. I use it on the dogs. When they jump up near my desk for a treat, some of them smell nasty. I give them just a little squirt and the smell is gone."

That was not the miracle I had hoped for, but it sure made for a funny story, and my knee never bothered me again. When I went for the follow up with my orthopedic doctor he was amazed by the healing and wanted to know what happened. I asked him if he believed in miracles.

"Let's just say I don't *not* believe in them," he said. My knee had been bone on bone in the x-ray, and now it was completely back to normal.

Someone else whom I'd been praying for without the desired results was my older sister, Mary. That summer, she had a seizure at work and was rushed to the hospital where a brain scan revealed a large tumor. We soon discovered it was glioblastoma, the same cancer my Aunt Patty had. We were all in shock.

I made a couple trips upstate to see her. I prayed endless rosaries for her healing, with particular emphasis on the third sorrowful mystery, "The Crowning of Thorns." On April 29, 2012, Mary went to her eternal reward, leaving behind a husband and five children. Frank and I, with the boys, drove upstate for the funeral. I was praying the rosary in the car as Frank was driving. When I reached the third sorrowful mystery, my sister's presence brushed over me. It was very unexpected, powerful and unmistakable. I felt that she wanted to tell me that she knew all the prayers that I had said for her during her illness. Mary, who never hesitated to express her gratitude toward others while she walked the earth, had found a way to thank me from her new perch. I wanted to write a poem to be read at the end of her funeral Mass, but I didn't have time. Frank told me he would watch the boys for the afternoon if I wanted to give it a try. We were staying with my cousin Marie Zea. I closed myself in her spare bedroom and wrote. Surprisingly, it took me only two hours...

Our Dearly Beloved Mary,
in you we witnessed acutely
life's contradictions:
strength in weakness,
peace in suffering

135

freedom in adhering.
Your being was Daily Bread
which you never withheld
from anyone.
You knew so much more
than you spoke.
You carried so much more
than you could hold.
And then, one day,
not too long ago,
you began to slowly go away.

We watched and waited
as petitions, near and far,
saturated your breathing space
begging for your release.
We had hoped it would be different.
We had never imagined an end like this.
But are you really gone for good?
We have our memories,
our treasured moments,
but how can we carry on
your legacy
when we know
we will never be
as good as you?

We've been dealt a mortal blow,
but still the earth turns and travels
its appointed path.
This very morning we awoke
expecting, not darkness,
but light.
So much so,
had the sun refused to show its face,

we would have been stunned
or worse
erased.

Mary, you have gone on.
We could say we are stunned
yet we know for certain
you never refused the way
you were given to run.
And you ran it with quiet force
and won!
And this victory
like everything else
you share with us.

Thank you, Mary!
We love you so much!

I knew Mary very well. She was only thirteen months older than me. We shared the same bedroom our whole childhood. I was not exaggerating when I wrote, "how can we carry on/your legacy/when we know/we will never be/as good as you?" She was an innocent lamb, and she died on Good Shepherd Sunday. Msgr. Albacete remarked, "Jesus took his little lamb home."

A week later, we were discussing the events at our breakfast table, and began talking about Jesus, the Good Shepherd. Micah and Martin were confused by the parable.

"Why would the shepherd leave ninety-nine sheep all alone just to find one?" Micah asked.

Frank's answer had all the weight of experience: "He didn't leave them alone. He left them with the other members of the herd." Then he added, "Jesus will never leave you alone. You will always have the community. And as long as you stay within the community, you will

137

be protected. And if you leave the herd, He will come and find you."

That May, Micah was preparing for his First Communion. The Director of Religious Education gave him a packet with all the material needed to make a banner with his name on it, which would be hung from his assigned pew. Any type of craft takes the shape of a burden for me, so I procrastinated until it was the day before, and then I had no time because I had to go out that evening. I promised Micah that I would make the banner when I came home. That night, as I was climbing the stairs of our apartment, feeling like the last thing I wanted to do was cut and paste letters and Eucharistic images on a big piece of felt, I sighed a quick prayer and thought, if that banner is made, I know that I'm married to a saintly man. I got to the top of the stairs, and there it was, finished and beautiful, lying on the dining room table. Frank told me that he had sat down with Micah, and they did it together.

"I Have Everything I Need, Right Here, Right Now"

Mary's passing was preparing our family for yet another big transition. Frank's liver doctor, who had prescribed the Hepatitis C treatment, had never bothered to have his liver scanned beforehand. But now Frank was starting to have pain, and he finally had an ultrasound, which uncovered lesions. It took months to get a proper diagnosis. There were tumors on his pancreas and liver, but they did not look like cancer. The surgical oncologist at St. Luke's-Roosevelt Hospital, who was an expert in the treatment of tumors of the liver and pancreas, called Frank "a mystery man."

At the end of June 2012, we packed up the car and headed to Honor's Haven Resort in Ellenville, New York. Frank was going to lead the annual CL East Coast Family Vacation. As we were leaving Brooklyn, Frank got a phone call from the doctor. He would have to come in for more tests, as the doctor suspected the tumors were malignant. Frank was driving as he received this news, and became very distracted. At the Verrazano Bridge toll booth, he squeezed into a lane of traffic, right in front of a big tractor trailer truck.

"Oh no!" Frank said, "He doesn't see me!"

It wasn't until we heard a big scape along the side of our car that the truck driver realized he had hit us. We spent hours stuck near the tollbooth, waiting for the police to come. When they finally arrived, they filled out an accident report and sent us on our way. By the time we reached the resort, dinner was almost over. Our friends surrounded us in the dining room as Frank gave them two pieces of bad news, first, we had had a car accident, and second, he probably had cancer. But being in the embrace of our friends in the community was like a healing balm. Frank became full of hope. When he spoke to our assembly the following morning, he told everyone, "I am facing this reality with certainty, not fear," and he credited his strength to the "great gift of love and friendship" he had received, something for which he constantly expressed his gratitude.

When we returned from vacation, Frank had more tests done. Our ninth wedding anniversary was coming up. We both felt an urgent need to celebrate it surrounded by our family and friends. At the last minute, I sent out an email asking them to come and have dinner with us at a Spanish restaurant we liked in Bay Ridge, Brooklyn. To our great joy and astonishment, almost everyone we invited was able to come. I realized that my and Frank's relationship was a gift for everyone, and private celebrations no longer made sense to me.

Soon we received news from the doctor that Frank's tumors appeared to be benign and operable, and Frank would most likely have surgery at the end of August. Frank went back to work, and I decided to take the boys upstate and spend time with my mother. Then, on August 20th, Frank called me saying that he had terrible pain in his side. I told him he had to go to the hospital, and I took the first flight I could find back to New York City.

Unfortunately, Frank's doctor was on vacation, so he was at the mercy of medical personnel who were not familiar with his case. They suspected he had kidney stones, and did not allow him food or drink for nearly three days. They also did not want to give him proper pain medication, considering he had a history of opioid abuse. When they came into his hospital room to draw blood, they poked him several times, but were unable to find a useable vein in his track marked, dehydrated arms. When they finally managed to run an IV line, they prepared Frank for a CT scan. He was wheeled in a hospital bed to a heavily air-conditioned hallway, where he waited for hours, still hungry, thirsty and in tremendous pain, and now shivering in a gown with just a sheet covering him. I held his hand. He looked at me with bright eyes and said, "I have everything I need, right here, right now." Those words rang in my soul every moment of every day in the days ahead.

The scan seemed to rule out kidney stones. The next step was a liver biopsy. On August 29th, Deacon Ramon Pons's birthday, we learned that Frank had neuroendocrine cancer, which had started in his pancreas and spread to his liver. Frank told Chris Bacich, "All my life, I've been terrified of cancer. But when I heard the news, the very first thing I thought of was Fr. Giussani suffering from Parkinson's and his affirmation from the Psalms: 'The Lord is my strength and my song!'" And he repeated: "The Lord is my song!"

Frank sent an email to his friends: "I am positive that the Lord has the final say in this, and I accept the cross that I am being asked to bear. I am in position, once again, to offer up everything to the Lord, with the certainty that He will take my suffering and turn it into blessings for everyone."

But Frank's acceptance of the cross did not mean that he was going to give up. On the contrary, I had never seen him so full of hustle and fight. He called our friend, Renzo Canetta, a cancer research doctor who knew the types of drugs that would work for this very particular cancer. Renzo drove all the way from Connecticut to come to our home and discuss Frank's treatment options. He had a big binder of notes and diagrams and explained everything to us in detail. Frank drank in the information and made an appointment with our in-network oncologist, who was ready to prescribe ordinary chemo while giving him only six months to live. Frank came back at him with all that Renzo had taught him, not just parroting the information, but displaying an understanding of the illness and the two possible drugs that could treat it. The doctor was stunned. He had to admit that he did not know enough about neuroendocrine cancer to properly treat Frank.

Renzo helped us to find the right oncologist: Dr. Peter Kozach of Mount Sinai Beth Israel Hospital in Manhattan. Dr. Kozach was listed among the "Best Doctors" in the June 2011 edition of *New York Magazine*. When we proposed Dr. Kozach to the medical director of the union health center, he granted Frank permission to be treated by an out-of-network doctor, but would not allow any tests to be done outside of the union health center. This made things very difficult and frustrating. Dr. Kozach had to rely on blood tests and scans taken at the clinic, and maddeningly outdated communication methods between the offices. Still, we knew Frank was in good hands. The first oncologist had told Frank he would be dead in six months. Dr. Kozach gave Frank hope. He told Frank that he was very healthy and strong, and prescribed one pill a day to shrink the tumors, hoping that Frank's cancer would be operable after the treatment.

His illness would mean that Frank had to sacrifice his position as leader of CL in New York. In an email dated October 23, 2012, Chris Bacich, head of CL in the USA, wrote, "Recognizing that Christ is asking Frank Simmonds to a particular witness right now through his condition struggling with cancer, I asked him to give up the responsibility of the community of New York." Frank had agreed. It was a painful decision for Frank, but he understood that he was in the fight for his life, and this did not allow him to expend energy elsewhere. Nevertheless, although organizational duties no longer fell to him, his life itself was becoming a witness that gave him great authority.

I received a very moving message from our friend, Ginnie Clancy:

> *My human heart breaks at the cross Frank and you, and all your family, are being asked to carry; my spirit quails at the prospect. I have the image of Frank carrying the cross in front of us over the Brooklyn Bridge, and I realize his openness to following Christ's path is being taken very seriously by the One who loves him. Frank's simplicity in front of the Christian proposal is radical, inspiring, life-giving— and it shakes me to the core to see the burden he has been deemed strong enough to carry because of his great love.*

Frank continued his treatment, and his tumors became smaller. After being out on disability for some months, Frank was able to go back to work. He told everyone, "Cancer did not create me and cancer needs permission to take me."

Fr. Peter Cameron, who had become editor of *Magnificat* magazine, and was one of the first people to encourage me as a poet, sponsored a reading of my poetry at St. Malachy's - The Actors' Chapel in New York City, that November 28th. Fr. Peter moderated the event, my brother-in-law, Jonathan Fields, played guitar, and my friend, David Galalis, projected his photography in the background. Frank came to help out in whatever way he could. Fr. Peter's assistant, Cathy Kolpak, was amazed by Frank's helpfulness, especially considering everything he was going through. At a certain point, while they were setting up, she realized she needed an extension cord. Frank ran out to Staples and bought one without missing a beat. During the reading, he took pictures and videotaped.

One of the poems that I chose to read proved to be a strange foreshadowing of the days to come:

"Queen Come Forth"

A queen
forever fruitful,
a kingdom
come forth,
Simeon sees
salvation
and sword.
He speaks
what a mother's heart
already knows.
The child
she lets go
is light,
light that will carry
flesh that will fall.
The prophet holds
what the queen brings forth,
and she will rule

144

with open eyes
the fall and the rise.[5]

[5] Rita A. Simmonds, "Queen Come Forth," *Magnificat Year of Faith Companion,* 2012, p. 128.

"I Don't Carry the Cross; the Cross Carries Me"

2013 was a very grace-filled year for Frank, and also, therefore, for all of us who knew him because he shared every grace that he was given with us. Physically, he was weak, and had lost some weight, but the cancer treatment seemed to be shrinking the tumors, so he was full of optimism and growing stronger in his faith. He spoke many times about how he was facing his illness as a husband and father of two small boys.

"When you're aware of who you are, that you belong to God, that you're His, everything changes. God is the Lord of my life, not cancer. I belong to Him, not to this disease." And he added, "I understand now that my life is a gift and that it is a road. I used to hate my life; all I wanted to do was escape it. Now I understand it's given to walk through because it leads to the Infinite. The only option for me is this walk. I am grateful for all the suffering, as it has a reason."

That Lent he waited with great anticipation, wondering if his diagnosis would prevent Chris Vath from asking him to carry the cross over the Brooklyn Bridge in the Good Friday procession. When the call finally came, Frank assured Chris that he was up for the task. "I don't carry the cross; the cross carries me," he said. But he also spent weeks preparing by praying, drawing closer to his friends, gathering the names of those who needed prayers, and even physically exercising. The day before the Way of the Cross, he went to the drugstore and bought adult diapers, as the cancer had made bathroom trips much more frequent.

The next morning, we got dressed and drove to St. James Cathedral in Brooklyn, where the procession would begin. While I rehearsed with the choir, Frank sat to the side of the altar, his face filled with pain and purpose, an expression I had come to know very well. He was soon joined by Fr. Rich Veras, and Bishop of Brooklyn, Nicholas DiMarzio. When Frank began walking with the cross, he was accompanied more closely than ever, with several friends directly behind him, the strong and protective figure of Thom Black to his left, and Renzo's son, Carlo Canetta, to his right.

When we stopped at the top of the bridge for the second station, Frank was led to the corner spot, near the railing, with the whole city of New York at his back. Knowing Frank's fear of heights, I moved from my place in the choir and stood beside him. While the Gospel was being read, Frank looked at me and said, "I love you." Then he kissed the wood of the cross, which he was holding very close to his face. It was such a deliberate act, and I remembered that, years before, he had refused to kiss the cross when our friend David had taken him to a Good Friday service with the Franciscan Friars of the Renewal. In that moment, I knew that Frank's walk with Christ was becoming extremely intimate, and that he was inviting me to share this intimacy with him.

"I'm Frank, Not Saint Francis"

When the walk had ended, Frank was exhausted but elated. It took him weeks to recover his physical strength, but his desire to share his experience was becoming greater and greater. He was still working, and when he came home from work in the morning, he would sit at the kitchen table, tired but eager to tell me what he was discovering through his illness. After a while, I started wishing other people could hear. One day I told him that his words should be recorded, so others could benefit from these treasures of grace. I ran to the other room and grabbed my video camera. And that's how *Frank Speak* started.

We made the first video on April 30, 2013, a month after Frank had led the Good Friday procession over the Brooklyn Bridge, and the day after we celebrated my sister Mary's First Anniversary Memorial Mass. In it, with characteristic humility about his own suffering ("pain that I'm sure that we all have to endure in our lives"), Frank described how the "meaning of my suffering is a freedom that I have never experienced before." He offered his suffering, and called on others to offer their suffering, for the world.

Good morning, everyone. I just wanted to mention one little thing today that I experienced which always starts for me with gratitude, gratitude for every second of my life, and just valuing every relationship, every bit of suffering that I go through because the meaning of my suffering is a freedom that I had never experienced before. It is the ability to freely open my heart and ask God to give meaning to pain – a pain that I'm sure that we all have to endure in our lives. [...R]ight now I'm enduring a great deal of pain and suffering, but I voluntarily carry my cross. And the freedom to not reduce this to an act that I'm doing to try to save myself, but to offer it fully, voluntarily, for everyone in this world, is a freedom that I wouldn't have gotten had I not experienced this suffering.

Every soul is precious...Sometimes we see people terrorizing and everything, but let's remember [that] when God created all of us, it was out of love, and every soul is worth more than everything—every star, every galaxy in the universe, and we have a freedom that no other animal, nothing else in this world has, and that's to realize that our strength and the love that we show to one another came from an original source: Our Lord and Savior Jesus Christ.

---

6 *Frank Speak 1* can be viewed at
https://www.youtube.com/watch?v=hOEhVcvyJ4A&t=2s

Peace to you, everyone, and as I suffer, and as you suffer, please join me in offering up our suffering for the world because you and I both know the world needs it very much, and we can participate by offering everything, being selfless, because we love. Thank you very much.

I posted the video on YouTube and emailed the link to several friends. The video quickly picked up hundreds of views from all over the country and even abroad. I received messages from people of all different religions, and even non-believers, all moved by Frank's testimony. Many asked if they could share the video with friends or family members who were undergoing various kinds of suffering. My friend Neil Bullock, who lived in Texas at the time, quoted Isaiah 53: "A man of sorrow and acquainted with grief" and called Frank's witness "powerful." My friend Jane Hubbard's sister asked if she could share the video with her grandmother and several others who "need a boost of encouragement." My friend, Ann Rawlins, expressed sorrow at seeing Frank in pain, yet was struck by his "shining example of class and deep faith." Our friend, Connie Pilsner, wrote, "I will remember this when I suffer. And I will try to remember this when I do not suffer because I do not want to take a moment for granted. But what I will remember most is that Christ's love is here."

On May 15th, Frank came home from work in the morning and sat at the kitchen table with me. We talked and had breakfast. Once again he started telling me what he was going through and how accompanied he felt. I told him he should make a second video so others could benefit from his experience, and he was happy to comply. This time he emphasized that his strength came from his dependency on "Something Greater than myself that loves me." This Power, he told anyone who would listen, "has called your name out, just like mine, above the stars in this universe, and out of love." Again he was careful to say that he was offering his suffering for everyone who suffered.

2013-05-15 Frank Speak 2[7]

Good morning. Today I'm a little bit more alert than the last video that I did a couple of weeks ago. I'm still the same, still in pain, but I'm still pushing along, keeping life simple, putting one foot in front of the other, and giving thanks for every day that I wake up in and my eyes open... I start from there and I move forward from that position.

I just wanted to mention a little bit about how I'm able to endure the [...] different hardships of life that I have right now. Believe me, it's not that I'm Mr. Strong or I've been doing exercise. It's not that at all. It's I depend. I get down on my knees and I beg. My life is important and it's at hand right now, and I'm in a position where surrender is a viable option for me, and I choose to surrender. But I'm not just surrendering to nothing; I'm surrendering to something, and that is my companionship, the companionship of Something Greater than myself that loves me, that allows me to lay my life down for you, and allows me to not just think of myself, but to think of every other person that's suffering in this world. I offer my suffering for them.

I'm not here for anyone's pity. I just want more people to accompany me on my walk. It's not really my walk actually; it's our walk, and I just want you

---

[7] https://www.youtube.com/watch?v=HnQm4OfVqWs&t=133s

to know that there is a name for the Higher Power. [...M]any people have a lot of different names, but I see it's God, Jesus Christ, [...] God's humanity [...]. I want to let you know that this Higher Power is with us. It's not far away in some parallel universe operating us like puppets. If that was the truth [...], and I felt alone without that Higher Power, this [situation] would be too much for me to handle.

So, my brothers and sisters, the love, the certainty, the faith that I have wasn't something I concocted on my own. It's a gift, and even in the midst of this cancer and chemotherapy, it has not convinced me that I'm alone. And I urge you never to be convinced that you're alone because there's a Power out there that is stronger than all of our problems that called your name out, just like mine, above the stars in this universe, and out of love. And we need to be aware of this because the world isn't getting easier; it's getting harder. Then you'll have to ask [...] yourself: Where is your faith?

[...M]y love is with you; my suffering is for you. Thank you very much.

In response to Frank's call to join him in offering up their suffering for the world, many friends came forward with their suffering. My friend Peggy Rosenthal and her husband George Dardess were both dealing with serious illnesses themselves. Peggy emailed me, "Please tell Frank that George & I watched his 2nd video last night during our Evening Prayer. He can count on us to accompany him in prayer along his journey."

People everywhere wanted to respond and correspond to Frank's request.

Frank was hoping that he would be able to have an operation on his liver to remove the tumors, but as time went by, it seemed the treatment was no longer working. A new scan revealed that the cancer had spread to Frank's lungs. It was beginning to hit home that the cancer was incurable.

Frank was losing weight and beginning to feel more pain, but he was still determined to fight. His sister, Emma, had watched his videos and became alarmed that Frank was resigned to death. He wanted to set the record straight. On the morning of May 30th, after he had worked all night, we sat at the kitchen table and, with an even greater sense of urgency, he made his third video. In it, he took care to emphasize the concreteness of his experience of support, and to eliminate any possible exaggerations about his piety, saying "my name is Frank. I am not St. Francis or anything like that." In addition to explicitly clarifying that his dependency was not resignation to death, he also wanted to make sure that everyone was clear on the first step of the journey he was making: acknowledging that life is a gift, and walking forward together toward something positive. "We are not defined by this world. We are defined by something greater."

2013-05-30 Frank Speak 3[8]

Good afternoon, everyone. My name is Frank Simmonds. [...] I am not St. Francis or anything like that. I lived a pretty hard life. [...] I spent so much time and so much money to buy happiness, just to find out that happiness was free. But also there's a certain amount of freedom even with this cancer

---

[8] https://www.youtube.com/watch?v=YgqxiQTzWv0&t=240s

diagnosis, because I feel that the cancer that I put myself through earlier in my life was even stronger than this cancer now. [...]

What I'm a part of is great. It's been the greatest gift that I could possibly have in my life: the knowledge...that I was created out of love by Something Greater than all the problems that the world has to offer. [...] I don't want to keep this gift to myself. I want to share it with the world, just like it's been shared with me.

So I'm asking you, if you're aware that your life is a gift, and that the reality that we deal with, we deal with not alone, but...with each other, then offer it to other people. Love without conditions, and pray. And even if you don't pray, acknowledge that you do not want to be part of the evil of the world, that you want to do something positive, not just for yourself and for your family, but for everyone. And for me, my way is offering up all my pain, my suffering, all of myself, for the world. I do this voluntarily, willingly; that is the greatest freedom that a person can ask for from my perspective, and I'm just asking you to join me.

My videos...are not a concession that I believe I'm dying...No. I die when God [decides]...I have no control over it, so what I do is I stay present. I stay in the present. I'm fine right now. Tomorrow's not guaranteed for anyone. No one knows if they're going to wake up tomorrow morning. But I did wake up this morning, and the first thing I said was, "Thank you for another day of opening my eyes." I offer this same thing to you that is my starting point of every day—gratitude, and I offer it up for you because I love everyone unconditionally.

You don't have to change who you are. All you have to do is walk with me...and we will make a difference in this world because we are not defined by this world. We are defined by something else greater.

Thank you very much and God bless you.

I sent an email around to friends and family with the link to Frank's video, and that same day we received a shocking response from our friend Fr. Richard Neilson:

Most impressive particularly as this day I was diagnosed as "being full of cancer". (I have my first radiation treatment next Tuesday.) What a great gift to offer to God in union with the Passion of his Son for all the world, for peace, for an end to all the dissension in the Church - for that unity Christ prayed for at the last supper, for the brotherhood of man. Frank, we were never more brothers than on this day.

Your presentation was excellent. May God reward you.

Love to Rita and the children and to yourself. June is the month of the Sacred Heart - may you all be greatly blessed by that Heart of Infinite love.

Pax et bonum. Fraternally in Christ,

Fr. Richard

Two days later, Giorgio Vittadini, the leader of the *Memores Domini* who had written to me from Milan to "follow my joy" when I first became friends with Frank, came to visit New York. The CL community gathered to meet with him in Manhattan. Frank got up and spoke before everyone. What he said in the space of a few short minutes summarized fifty years of life experience: the man from the past who had wanted to throw his life away, and the man today, who, despite his weakness, experienced God's presence so powerfully that he wasn't worried about his own survival, and his only fear was not having enough time left to give.

You know, [...] the more that I strive to have the answers, the more that I find out that I don't have the answers, and the more that it connects me with Something Greater than myself... A guy that wanted to take his life years ago is in the fight for his life now. And...I'm fortunate that I was able to live this contrast: that I could see the guy that wanted to give his life up, and told God that his life was nothing and it wasn't a privilege to have, and now I'm facing something where my life is at stake, and I'm standing here depending. Depending not on myself, because I'm a wreck, I'm no strong guy... But I know where my strength comes from; it's not from me. I depend... And it's not in some abstract way. It's not like I'm waiting for God somewhere off in some wilderness [...] to shoot lightning bolts down. No! No! He's right here. This is my reality, right here. He's part of this... I didn't ask for cancer, but I have it, and I'm still standing in front of it, and I'm still depending. I'm not jumping out a window. I'm taking one step at a time. I'm walking towards whatever reality offers. I'm not trying to run from it.

What gave me the strength? Before, when I had all these problems, I wanted to kill myself. Now I'm standing in front of the same difficulties, but I'm walking forward...

What's your true love? This cancer is asking me, "Who are you, Frank? Who are you? Because I can make you like Job. I can make you want to curse God." Yet that's not happening. I don't know why. I can't write it down, I can't put it in a pill and give it to anybody. I'm just living this way, and I'm amazed. I'm amazed, because it happens from Something Greater than me. Because I'm not that great. I walk outside, and trip over my own feet. But [...] I'm standing before something so deadly and so scary, [and yet] I'm not worried about my survival; I want to give. [...]

And I have never felt alone. I've always felt accompanied through everything, even from the first day they told me: "It's not your kidney, it's THIS!" I'm like, "Whaaaat?!" But that "what" only lasted a second, because I went through the streets. I went through being shot at, trying to be killed, trying to kill myself... That kind of cancer is greater than this kind of cancer. I was carried through, I was helped through that. [...] So I try to keep my life as simple as possible. I depend, and I just walk forward.

Frank also took the opportunity to comment on what he was intending to do with the *Frank Speak* videos:

So, if you do see those videos that I've been putting out on YouTube, I'm just trying to say: Listen, I'm in a position now where I can fail [...], but I'm going to take what I have and I'm going to offer it up. And if I'm going to offer it up, to whom?! Whom am I going to offer it to? My wife?! Is she going to change everything?! No, I'm offering it to something much greater than the sum of all the things, [...] because I know He can take this, and He can bless everyone else with it. And I think from that perspective I'm a blessed man.

After hearing this, Vittadini remarked to everyone there that Frank's life put all of us at a crossroads:

Frank is a miracle. Every one of us knows his story, and now, after tonight, you have to choose: Is Frank a dream? Is Frank a crazy man with hallucinations[...]? Or is Frank someone able to look at his destiny, and, in front of his cancer, able to understand that the meaning of his life, and the answer to the questions that his life brings to him, are greater than his survival? [...]

If you don't believe that Christ is a presence, you have to destroy Frank; you have to say that it's not true; you have to forget him[...]. You have to say that he didn't speak – instead, he spoke. We saw this fact, and in front of this fact, as in the beginning, as in front of Christ, we have to choose: Is this true, or not? [...And] if you say that it's not true, [...] you have to explain to us here why you think that a man in this position is able to think about something other than his disease[...].

Today [we saw] a miracle in the strict sense. A miracle means something that happens not because human beings or nature are able to build it. [...] It's something connected to the mystery; I can't explain it in a logic[al] way. This is the victory of Christ. This is the glory of Christ. Just one guy like Frank is the demonstration of the resurrection, because you can't destroy it.

Frank's witnesses helped many people, and it helped him, too, to be able to talk about his experience, and to hear what it meant to others. Giorgio's response proved to be a particular point of strength and certainty for Frank in the difficult days ahead, when the disease seemed to be progressing. He was experiencing more pain in his abdomen and losing a lot of weight. He had also developed swollen ankles and shortness of breath. His oncologist was concerned that the cancer was affecting Frank's heart. Tests revealed that his right heart valves were damaged. The union cardiologist prescribed a beta-blocker to lessen the strain on Frank's heart.

"Suffering Has a Meaning"

At the end of August, our friends Thomas and Patricia Byrne invited us out to their home in Montauk, Long Island for some rest and relaxation. They cooked delicious meals for us and entertained Micah and Martin. Their son, Gregory, took the boys fishing and boogie boarding, and played baseball with them. Their daughter, Eleanor, sat and listened to Frank speak about his life.

On the afternoon of August 27, 2013, our hosts offered to stay with the boys so Frank and I could have some time alone. We went to the beach, and Frank took out his video camera and filmed *Frank Speak 4* himself, as he stood in front of the ocean at the end of the island where he was born and raised. Wearing sunglasses against the brilliant sunlight, silhouetted against the clear, blue sky, in the video Frank is unable to keep the smile from his lips as he talks about the greatness of God and creation:

"I think of the times when my life was so bad I didn't even believe I was a human being anymore," he said. "Yet out of my heart, even in the midst of the worst circumstances, a poem came out." He recited "Lord, Show Me the Way," the poem he had written over thirty years before, in a prison not far from where we stood. He remarked: "In the midst of the deepest, the darkest, the most painful things – your freedom being taken – you're exposed to another freedom: the freedom of saying *yes* or *no* to an invitation from something greater than yourself." He acknowledged that his struggle was becoming more intense, but re-affirmed: "The joy that's been given to me cannot be taken, and I offer every bit of every struggle that I have…to the Lord for you." The ocean seemed to inspire him:

2013-08-27 Frank Speak 4[9]

Although I'm not able to love completely, I'm being led in a direction to experience love in its ultimate form: The love of the Creator who created such beautiful things as the ocean, the sky, the sun, the forest, the trees. Just as you see the many grains of sand, so too are we counted and we lay in God's hand. Yes, one day we will all stand on the precipice of extinction, but does it end there? Search your heart and the answer will be there. It will be clear as it could be. It was there before you were even born, and the sacrifices that we make are to something greater than our minds could ever imagine. We are children of the Infinite and the only thing He asked was for us to live the life that we have, and for us to love each other as we love ourselves. And in this way, you too are my brothers and my sisters, and I love you very much, and I offer everything for you. Thank you very much.

---

[9] https://www.youtube.com/watch?v=6-a5aTJ4EvY

After our mini-vacation on Long Island, Frank and I were invited to Pittsburgh, PA to participate in a cultural festival organized by our friends Stephen and Suzanne Lewis. I was invited to read a few poems, and Frank to give a witness, which he titled, "Suffering has a Meaning." Frank's sister, Althea, came to stay with the boys. We picked up our friend, Raquel, and were off. It took over six hours to drive there, and Frank was not feeling well. I felt as though I should have asked Suzanne for a plane ticket, but once we arrived, Frank's condition seemed to improve. I was very happy to meet up with an old friend whom I hadn't seen in years, Fr. Vincent Nagle, of the Priestly Fraternity of Saint Charles Borromeo, who happened to be the keynote speaker. Fr. Vince is a passionate and intense man, who often says and does the unexpected. After Frank delivered his hour-long talk, Fr. Vincent was the first person to approach him. From across the room, I saw Frank place his right hand on Fr. Vincent's forehead, then bend down and touch his feet, and then touch him on each shoulder. I later asked him what he was doing.

"I was giving him a blessing."

"Why?"

"Because he asked me for one."

Early that evening, I presented a few of my poems. I read so slowly, I thought I must have put everyone to sleep. I ended with "Greeting the Seasons"[10] which describes the coming and going of the four seasons. It ends with a couplet, which I was feeling more deeply than ever:

---

[10] Rita A. Simmonds, "Greeting the Seasons," *Greeting the Seasons: Poems for the Holidays*, 2016, p. 47.

Go nature, rhyme and round the "why?"
Just give us time to say "good-bye."

Before we left, Frank asked Fr. Vincent for *his* blessing. Frank was experiencing more shortness of breath and was having trouble walking any distance without getting winded. On the ride back to Brooklyn, I was anxious, and Frank was irritable. When we finally arrived home, although Frank was exhausted, he wanted to show his sister the photos we'd taken. He knew he had lost fifty pounds since he had started his treatment, but he didn't realize how thin and frail he'd become until he downloaded the pictures onto his computer. "I look so weak, like I can barely stand, and my wife has to hold me up." He broke down in tears.

It was very difficult for me to see my husband struggle emotionally. He had always been my rock, even while his physical condition deteriorated. But now he was becoming irrational and critical. He would get angry very easily and storm out of the house without telling me where he was going. When I questioned his behavior, he told me that I was the one with the problem, not him. One thing that I knew for sure was that this man who was constantly blaming me for everything, was NOT my husband. What really convinced me was the day he looked at our son, Martin, who was peacefully eating his breakfast, and said to him, "Something's wrong with you." Martin turned his head, thinking he was talking to someone behind him. That's when I knew I had to do something to stop Frank. I sat him down at the kitchen table and said, "Honey, if I accept all the blame for everything that you tell me is wrong with me, will you stop accusing me?"

He thought about it for a long while, and looked very confused. Finally he shook his head and said, "No, and I don't know why."

I spoke with medical professionals and friends and begged for help. Some thought Frank was experiencing the trauma of knowing he had an incurable disease. Others blamed me, saying I put too much stress on Frank and should have asked for a plane ticket to Pittsburgh instead of subjecting him to the long car drive. I felt that these could have been contributing factors, but I also knew that Frank's behavior had started to change once he began taking the heart medication. Others agreed that mixing the heart medicine with the chemotherapy, painkillers, and medicine to increase his appetite, could most certainly have altered Frank's mood.

We managed to have Frank's medication adjusted, and as soon as we did, I noticed a change for the better. On September 24, 2013, he stood in our living room in a tank undershirt and jeans, with a cross and Luigi Giussani medal that Suzanne Lewis had given him, around his neck. This time, it was he who asked me to film him:

2013-09-24 Frank Speak 5[11]

Good morning, everyone. [...] I just wanted you to see I'm still standing. I'm still smiling. The grace of the Lord is with me, and it's not my strength that gets me through everything; it's my faith.

[...] I'm not here to preach to you. I'm just here to tell you about my life[...]. This is not like someone's fake story. I am living this life. Do I know how? No. I'm amazed that a guy whose mother and father and brother have died of cancer, now is carrying the cross of cancer himself and is able to face it differently than he even thought was possible.

---

[11] https://www.youtube.com/watch?v=oO9hHaR8ImI&t=39s

So I'm asking you to join me where Christ is leading me. [...W]hen I've been given the ability and the awareness to know that my suffering can be offered for you, from love that was given to me, it became even deeper of a suffering, but it became suffering with a meaning.

Frank was always concerned for the suffering of others, and here he interrupted the video with a shout-out for his friend Fr. Nielson, in his own struggle with cancer ("I love you, man") and everyone else who was listening, with their own specific challenges: "I don't have it as bad as many other people."

Although Frank's cancer was terminal, he did not see his life as fundamentally different from others, and he wanted to remind everyone that, even if "some of us are experiencing it at a different intensity right now, [...] one day our eyes are all going to close." The one thing that was given to all of us in this "walk towards the Infinite," he said, with "Grace and love." And he added: "we can do our part too, we can offer up our suffering."

Despite cancer, heart problems, and all the things that have been thrown at me, I'm grateful. If my eyes didn't open up tomorrow, I would have died a happy man because I'm grateful for the life that I have, and I hope you are, too.

"The Torture Never Stops"

My fiftieth birthday was coming up. Friends and family members asked me if I wanted to have a party. I told them "no," but as the days went by, I regretted it. My sister Naomi came through at the eleventh hour and helped Frank plan a "surprise" party for me at the Greenhouse Café, the same restaurant where she had celebrated her 40th birthday the year before. My mother and sister Regina came in from out of town. My brothers couldn't come because my niece's boyfriend, Brian, had passed away after battling the same cancer Frank had. Still, it was a simple but very beautiful gathering. Raquel Isaza, Rachel Oberman and Tiffiny Gulla decorated the room with autumn leaves, Fr. Rich Veras told funny stories about our college days at Hofstra University, and Stacy and George Lugo showed off some dance moves. Frank even got up and danced with me, which was a big sacrifice, not only because of his health, but because he didn't like to dance.

A week later I sent out this email:

Thank you for your love for me which has not gone away after so many years--my mother since before I was born, my family, friends (very old and not so old, but very true), my husband who is my rock...his love for me, my love for him pushes us on to embrace the

Mystery more and more (sometimes with thorns!).
[...] I remain stubborn in my desire to repeat again
and again the prayer to Our Lady, "Pray for us
sinners NOW." And even as you read this, know that
she is praying for you NOW. My life has been marked
forever by this knowledge...the power of maternal
prayers...

Tiffiny Gulla, whom I met at a CL meeting in Brooklyn in 2006, had taught me a lot about Mary's love. She, too, was battling a terminal illness, scleroderma, which she was diagnosed with after being in lower Manhattan when the Twin Towers fell on September 11, 2001. The doctors told her she wouldn't live ten years, and she had already surpassed that, although the disease had done a great deal of damage: she no longer had fingers, her toes were knotted, and she had a large wound on her elbow that never healed and difficulty swallowing. But she also had a great love for life and a very strong faith. Her friendship, prayers and offerings were an invaluable source of strength to me and Frank.

Tiffiny hated nicknames. Frank was the only one who could get away with calling her "Tiff" or "the Tiffster." Somehow, people always knew that his nicknames were a sign of love. When our friends Michael and Heather O'Neill had their son Callixtus, Frank asked, "How's my man, Lixy?" Another time, he approached Sr. Marie Therese of the Sisters of Life, and said, "Hey, Sis!" Not even Timothy Cardinal Dolan took offense when, after a memorial Mass for Fr. Giussani at St. Patrick's Cathedral, Frank embraced him and said, "What's up, Card?"

Frank had funny names for most of our family members and friends. He called our friend, Ruby, "Ruby Roo." My sister Naomi was "Nelly Weller," her husband Ken, "Ken Diggity Dog." My sister Susan was "Suzy

168

Wooz," and Regina was "Genie." When Micah was a baby, he called him "Poopasurus Rex" and "Micahpotomus." He called Martin "Marnie." He never called me Rita unless he was angry. Usually he called me "Ma" or "Mama." When he thought I was being too rigid or judgmental, he called me "Rebecca of Sunnybrook Farm" after the character played by Shirley Temple in the movie of the same name. When I got upset or nervous, he would say, "Chicken Little, the sky is falling," or, from Bugs Bunny, "Brody, get ahold of yourself!"

Frank also had an endearing phrase for our friend Rachel Oberman who lived with her husband, Ted, and their five daughters, in downtown Brooklyn, just a couple blocks from the union health clinic. We would often stop by their house after Frank had a test or saw one of his doctors.

"How are you doing, Frank?" she would ask, with a big grin on her face, knowing that he was going to sing a line from Frank Zappa's "The Torture Never Stops."

And, as time went on, the torture did, indeed, seem to increase. There was still no resolution to Frank's heart trouble, as the union cardiologist felt that Frank was not a candidate for surgery, so he would have to manage his condition by cutting salt out of his diet, taking pills to get rid of the fluid buildup, and elevating his feet as much as possible.

At the end of November, amidst all the turmoil, I published my first book of poems, *Souls and the City*. One of the poems, "RainBow," recalls the days when Frank was healthy, and we had normal marital spats.

We were having
our Friday night fight
accompanied only by R&B
(always louder than I'd like)

169

as we drove uptown
slotted inside three teeming lanes,
the gray sky
all the while
spraying fall rain
as it had been for days
and days
and days.
The car stops and starts
to the R&B cool—
the you I can't break.
"It's almost over,"
is all you say.
An archway's unleashed
in the sun
and the blues
and the tapering rain.[12]

"Pruned Tree in Mid May" shadows Frank's deteriorating health:

This tree
has lost its leaves.
Twigs all clipped
it sticks the air
in fruitless symmetry.

When all the others
shimmer green
this one stands
with knobby hands
to twist the fall of spring.
Baldness
always shocks the eye,

---

[12] Rita A. Simmonds, "RainBow," *Souls and the City*, 2013, p. 33.

but on a tree
it poses dread—
brown bones against the sky.[13]

The poem, "Gambling" describes the days before we were married, when Frank and I used to meet in a coffee shop in Harlem which also sold scratch-off lottery tickets.

It's the truth I trust that's in your touch,
the fortune in your change.[14]

How much Frank had changed! What a fortune I'd gained.

At the end of December, Naomi's husband, Ken, proposed we make a novena (nine days of prayer) to Fr. Giussani for Frank's healing. On the ninth day, New Year's Eve, Frank woke up at night and started vomiting. It didn't stop for hours. I was so frightened that I wanted to call the ambulance, but he wouldn't let me. I prayed the novena prayer to Fr. Giussani. When I realized it was the final day, I became furious! "How could you do this to us! Why aren't you helping us? We've been asking and asking, *begging* for Frank to be cured, and this is what happens? You are my father. I have asked for bread and you have given me a stone! I asked for fish and you gave me a serpent, and this serpent is striking me and poisoning your son."

The next morning was New Year's Day, 2014. Frank was sleeping soundly after the night of horror. I called my friend, Janene Parranello, to find out if her son, Anthony, whom I'd been preparing for baptism, wanted to go to Mass. I had known Janene and Eric and their son, Anthony, since Martin had started pre-K in 2010 and they

---

[13] *Souls and the City*, p. 41.
[14] *Ibid*

were both in the same class. Janene had a brain injury from being shot in the head in a drive-by shooting at Kings Plaza in Brooklyn when she was seventeen years old. She was fortunate to get married and have a little boy years later, but she continued to suffer a lot of pain, partial blindness and seizures. One day when Frank went to pick Martin up from school, Janene had a seizure in the schoolyard. Frank ran to her aid and walked her home. We became friends, and that's when I learned that Janene wanted Anthony to be baptized. But that morning, Janene did not want Anthony to go to Mass. "But let me ask you a question," she said, "Have you ever seen a dead body?"

"What?"

"Eric hasn't moved all night."

I knew that Eric had health problems, but I never expected that he would die at the age of thirty-nine. I didn't know what to say or do. I had to wake Frank up.

He took the phone. "Janene, you have to call the ambulance."

She didn't want to.

"I'll be right there," Frank said.

We got the boys dressed and walked over to her apartment. I got Anthony out immediately and took him and our two boys to St. Mary's church. We were there several minutes before Mass started, so we prayed the rosary. Frank called and told me that Eric was dead; he was waiting with Janene for the ambulance.

Days later, I wondered if Frank's tremendous suffering on New Year's Eve was what Eric needed for his journey. I felt as though the novena prayer *was* answered. I recalled what Frank said months earlier, "My fear isn't fear of dying; my fear is not being able to give more to the world at this point. I'm not worried about my survival; I want to give." Frank was a victim soul. He was fulfilling his destiny.

At Eric's funeral Mass, when his coffin was being wheeled down the aisle, little Anthony, who was following behind it with his mother, looked up at me as he passed and said, "You know what, Rita? My dad is going to be so proud of me when I get baptized!"

Eric's death was followed by another. On January 19, my Aunt Patty Davis passed away. She had lived four years with brain cancer, and had joined Frank in offering her sufferings for the world.

When Frank recovered from what seemed to have been a terrible flu, he developed a lung infection. The doctor gave him antibiotics and steroids, which made him feel much better. After his follow up appointment, we met his friend Earl Nixon, whom Frank knew from the streets of East New York, and Earl's girlfriend Mary. We had lunch together at Checkers Chicken near the health clinic. It was such a joyful reunion, after so much suffering, I was moved to write this poem:

"Fast and Lasting Food"

Toward the fat smell of fast food
we moved like a herd
coming in from the cold and congealing rain
dragging humanity
hungry for French fries and friendship
waiting in long lines to gain
some comfort covered with ketchup.
We packed our parka-ed selves into a booth
flattened the paper which wrapped our food
and retold our lives between mouthfuls
growing more alive with surprise
having broken every commandment

173

how we survived.
We were delivered from evil
and in the breaking of the bun
recognized a hallowed childhood
and a Father who is good
to everyone.[15]

---

[15] Rita A. Simmonds, "Fast and Lasting Food," *Greeting the Seasons: Poems for the Holidays*, p. 41, 2016.

"I Found Strength in Depending"

Every year, some friends of ours in Communion and Liberation organize a three-day cultural event in Manhattan, with talks and multi-media presentations, called the New York Encounter. In 2014, the Encounter's theme was *The Time of the Person; The Origins of a People*. Frank was invited to speak on its January 17th panel entitled "Life Belongs to Something Greater" with Fr. Samir Khalil Samir, SJ, Professor of Islamic Studies at the University of Saint Joseph in Beirut, and our own Msgr. Lorenzo Albacete. Frank told his conversion story to an audience of over 900 people.

At the end of his talk, he spoke about his experience of studying the writings of Fr. Giussani and growing in the awareness of belonging:

> *My wife [...] told me about Fr. Giussani and showed me his book. I opened it up and was like, What?! You gotta be a Harvard grad to read this book! But you know what? All of those words...that I thought I couldn't understand? I started to experience them. And when I started to experience them, they became real [...]. I found strength in depending on something greater than myself, which allowed me to see the meaning of my life and its contrasts [...]. I'm*

175

able to sit here and say, Yes! It is the time of the person. I am a person, and these are my people, and I'm proud of that [...] We do this together. This encounter is for all people. It's for all people. I'm in love with everyone. But first I had to fall in love with myself and value my life.

I had the opportunity to speak with many old friends who were in town for the weekend. One was Tara Sareen. She looked me in the eyes and asked, "But how are *you* doing, Rita." I broke down and cried.

After the New York Encounter, Frank wrote a reflection on his experience:

The journey that we are on is not just a regular encounter. It's an encounter that generates a newness, an encounter that is far beyond our preconception or our limited perception [...]. The theme of this Encounter: the time of the person; the origins of a people, connects you directly to Christ's humanity and the certainty that only requires an open heart. This encounter is not just for us or for one person; it's for everyone; it's an invitation to the recognition of a gaze and the gentle yet powerful embrace of the Source of everything. In this way, there is nothing abstract about our faith because the unity of a people who understands the embrace of Christ's humanity is the very core of our existence. This allows us not to walk in fear of reality, but to embrace it together as a people. This accompaniment is not generated by ourselves, in the same way that we cannot affirm ourselves. [...W]e became an extension of a Presence, therefore, not looking at our differences, but at the one thing that links us together, what we have in common, and this is part of the Mystery, the curiosity, the seriousness, yet the tenderness we have as a people [...].

Your brother in Christ,

Frank (Simmonds)

In spite of Frank's weakening condition, he still went to work and, when he came home, spent as much time as he could with the boys. Martin's friend had a Mohawk haircut, and he asked Frank if he could have one, too, so Frank cut and styled Martin's hair and sent him to school feeling very proud and happy. But when Martin came home, he was almost crying. "Can you believe the kids laughed at me? Even after I told them my father is sick and it was very hard for him to cut my hair, they still laughed at me."

For Martin's eighth birthday, we invited his friends and their families bowling. Frank bowled two games with the kids, and then we had pizza and ice cream cake together. It was a joyful celebration.

In the coming months, Frank's ankles became so swollen that the only footwear that still fit was bedroom slippers, which he had to wear out in the snow and to work. Frank's oncologist was becoming increasingly frustrated with the union health clinic's lack of urgency towards Frank's worsening heart condition. He finally told us that, unless something was done about Frank's regurgitating valves, he would no longer treat Frank.

We left the oncologist and went directly to the clinic. Frank walked into the director's office, sat in front of him, put his swollen ankles up on the desk and said, "Doc, unless you do something about my heart, I'm going to die."

The doctor was shocked by the severity of the edema. He told Frank, "Find a heart surgeon, and I'll sign off on it."

We did some research and found Dr. Sunil Abrol at Maimonides Hospital in Brooklyn. Again, we had to abide by the rules of our health insurance provider and have all the tests done at the clinic. Dr. Abrol laughed when we hand delivered Frank's chest x-ray. "I haven't seen one of these in years," he said, taking the large film out of its envelope. Dr. Abrol was very compassionate and accommodating. He told Frank that he needed to have his right heart valves replaced, and that he would perform the surgery pending Dr. Kozuch's approval. We later discovered that Dr. Abrol agreed to perform the operation on the condition that Frank would live at least three months.

"Either He Exists or this Is a Big Scam"

That Lent, March 5th to April 17th, 2014 (the forty days before Easter), turned out to be a season of intense prayer, sacrifice and conversion.

Frank's surgery was scheduled for March 12th. People from all over the world were praying for the best possible outcome. Frank made his sixth video from his hospital bed at Maimonides. Looking weary but serene in his hospital gown, talking over the blare of someone watching television in the same room, and patiently gathering his thoughts after the frequent interruptions of passing hospital staff, he delivered a message in which, even in the face of a serious operation, he was clearly thinking about others:

2014-03-11 Frank Speak 6[16]

Good morning. I'm sitting here in Maimonides hospital. I'm about to go in tomorrow and have [...] open heart surgery. [...] I've been urging everyone to take their pain and suffering and offer it up for the world. At this moment I'm living that very thing.

---

[16] https://www.youtube.com/watch?v=Tas-L6SSbvE

Even at this moment when things look hard, I still say that my suffering has a meaning, and that meaning is being able to offer it up for the world, not just one person in particular, but the world, because all things were made by God.

He even put in a plug for my second book of poems, *Bitterness and Sweet Love*, which I dedicated to "my loving husband who loves the cross of Christ." He urged everyone to go out and buy a copy. He then expressed his awareness of the seriousness of the operation: "We live, our life is but a minute, like a whisper, then we come in the face with an unknown entity called death." But greater than this was his awareness of the fact that he was not alone:

I've encountered another entity...my faith in my Lord and Savior, Jesus Christ [...] Never have I felt more accompanied in hardship as I do today because the love of God is with me, and it's not manifested as an abstract God that sits up in heaven...but I see God smiling at me as I look in everyone's face... Everyone's a gift. Each person that I encounter is another opportunity to another, greater relationship with my brothers and sisters.

Frank explained that, once we acknowledge the fact that we do not control our lives, "Something else greater has to have us in an embrace."

I'm in this embrace right now, and I just want you to know that before I close my eyes, before they put the anesthesia into my body, the love that I have, the love that has been given to me for my fellow brother and sister, I will lay everything down for you. Why? Because I have to? No. I voluntarily lay my life down for you, and, yes, you can take this personally...For each and every person that sees this video, please understand God is greater than all the problems of our world and some, and I ask Him to have mercy on us because a lot of times we do things we don't even know we do.

Before Frank went into surgery, Fr. Francis, the hospital chaplain at Maimonides came and gave Frank Holy Communion and anointed him. Frank began feeling very dizzy. I was concerned and asked the nurse practitioner to call Dr. Abrol, who came immediately. He told Frank to try and relax as much as possible. "I got people all over the world praying for the success of this surgery, Doc," Frank said.

Frank was cheerful and confident throughout all the prepping procedures. When he went into surgery, I went to the waiting room and watched the tracking board's electronic screen count down the minutes. Julio and Miguelina Jimenez and John and Molly Ronan came and sat with me. When the operation was over, I hurried down to the intensive care unit and waited outside the double doors for the surgeon. When the medical team came out, an exhilarating breeze came with them. One of the attending approached me, smiling from ear to ear: "I haven't seen a surgery go that well in a really long time."

I was permitted into Frank's room in the ICU. He had a tube down his throat, but was struggling to communicate. I gave him a pen and notebook. He wrote, "Morphine does nothing." There was a male nurse in the room who had the sniffles, maybe from allergies. He kept wiping his nose with the back of his hand. I was becoming very nervous. I finally had to ask him to wash his hands.

Dr. Abrol came in and checked everything. He told me that the surgery had gone very well. I expressed concern over the dosage of the pain medication, and he made sure that Frank had what he needed.

Frank was recovering well, but I was anxious and compulsively disinfected all the surfaces in his room with hospital wipes. "There's no stopping my wife," he said, weakly, with a smile, to no one in particular. After six days of excellent care, he was ready to come home. He was thinner and much weaker, but no longer had swollen ankles. As we drove through Brooklyn, he asked me to pull over near a deli. "Why?" I asked.

"Never mind. Just pull over."

He wouldn't take "no" for an answer. I stopped the car, and he got out and went into the deli. After a couple minutes, he came out with a lottery ticket.

Frank had a lot of new medications added to what he was already taking. As the days went by, I hoped his appetite would come back and he would gain some weight and some strength. He wanted mint chocolate chip ice cream, so I started adding it to his nutrition shakes. It seemed that was all he ate for months.

Fr. Rich had asked me to do a poetry reading on March 21st for his parish's Lenten series at St. Rita's on Staten Island. Frank was still recovering from his surgery, but wanted to be present in some way, so he made a video from his bed, which was projected at the end of the reading. He was weak but joyful and smiling:

I'm amazed that despite all the things that reality has presented in front of us—good, bad, indifferent—I'm really amazed that my wife could write such beautiful, inspired poems, and would even take the time out to dedicate this book to me.

The one thing we always have to keep in mind is that we've been given more beautiful gifts than we've

*gotten pain and sorrow, and that's because He is
greater than all the problems that we've had.*

*I hope that these poems inspired you as much as they
inspired me. I'm a truly gifted man, and we are a
truly gifted people. I hope that when you leave, the
positivity and blessings of God will follow you.*

The reading went very well. I read poetic reflections on
the Fourteen Stations of the Cross, accompanied by my
friend, Raquel's, paintings. One poem, in particular,
deeply resonated with my experience, and would continue
to echo in my soul in the days ahead:

"Eleventh Station: Jesus Is Nailed to the Cross"

*His body's been stretched to the limitless,
wrought iron holding human hands and feet.
The inscription claims this attraction is "King."
The Queen accepts.
She is strong but not steeled,
wounded by nails
her heart
to his heel.
She fights with him for life
with every labored breath.
His flesh is pressed
and spasms in her flesh.*

*This child she's borne has suffered, will die
yet the sorrowful mother is blessed to conceive
what hatred and haste can't fix on a tree.
The Kingdom of Love is of freedom and seed.[17]*

---

[17] Rita A. Simmonds, "Eleventh Station: Jesus Is Nailed to the
Cross," *Bitterness and Sweet Love: The Way of the Cross and other
Lenten Poems,* 2014, p. 12.

The hope that we had for Frank's recovery was soon dashed. Two days after my reading, he was rushed to the hospital because he was having trouble breathing. We waited in the emergency room at Maimonides, amid a sea of people on stretchers and cots, for almost two days. It was my first experience witnessing such a heavy concentration of suffering and commotion, with people speaking all different languages and a constant flow of incoming wounded. I felt like I was in a MASH unit, and kept expecting to see Alan Alda, unshaven in a red bathrobe, walk through the double doors. But this was not a sitcom; it was real life. Frank was in a lot of pain and distress, and I desperately needed to see a familiar face that could help me navigate the chaos while we waited for Dr. Abrol. I called our friend, Francesco Rotatori, a cardiologist, and he came right away. He watched the technicians hook Frank up to various machines. It was clear that Frank had fluid around his heart and lungs. I had to repeatedly haggle with the nurses to get him the proper pain medication. How much more could he take, I wondered. The line from my poem kept coming back to me, "His body's been stretched to the limitless."

My mother was taking care of the boys, and she let everyone know what was happening. Soon there was a huddle of family and friends outside the white curtain, where Frank lay waiting for surgery. Dr. Abrol made sure that Frank would be operated on as soon as possible.

This second surgery was extremely difficult for Frank. He had to be awake while the doctor cut into his chest to remove the two liters of fluid that had accumulated there. Again, the pain medication failed to work.

"Doc, I'm feeling this!" Frank cried out. Then he remembered his promise to offer up all his pain and suffering, and began calling out people's names. He thought of the "billions and billions" of people in need of his prayers, and offered his pain for them.

After the surgery, Frank still had to have another procedure to drain the fluid from his lungs. He was so weak, he could barely speak, but he did say, with strength and conviction, "Tell Tiffiny that I love her." Our friend Tiffiny's illness was getting progressively worse as well, and the two of them were profoundly united in offering their suffering for the salvation of the world.

One day Frank told me that he had had a vision. Tiffiny was lowered from the sky on a rope, twirling around like a ballerina and having a lot of fun, no longer disfigured from the scleroderma. Frank watched her for a while, full of joy at how much she was enjoying herself. Then she slowly started to be lifted up into the sky, still spinning at the end of the rope.

"Tiff, where are you going?" Frank said.

"You can't come yet." She said, "It's not your time." And she was gone.

When Frank relayed the vision to me, he didn't know that, before Tiffiny had gotten sick, she was a dancer. He was very surprised. I understood that the vision was for me. As long as Tiffiny was alive, Frank would be alive. This took away a lot of my fear and gave me great comfort. Tiffiny ended up outliving Frank, but the comfort of this vision remained. By the time Frank was in his final days, I had reached a place that made it possible to conceive of letting him go.

A couple days after having his lungs drained, Frank was discharged. After recovering some of his strength, on April 2, 2014, sitting at the kitchen table, he made his seventh video. His weakened condition was apparent. He wanted to share his experience with everyone:

2014-04-02 Frank Speak 7 [18]

Good morning my brothers and sisters! It's been a little while, actually it's been a couple of weeks since I went in for my operation on my heart in which I got two valves replaced. I went in confident because I knew that whatever suffering I was going to go through I had already offered it up for the world, and it turned out to be a little more suffering than I thought.

Here, he was referring to the fact that, while the doctors believed he was under anesthesia, the pain medication was not working, and the pain was extreme.

I still, once again, offered it up for the whole world, and [...] a few people that I have that are constantly on my heart, and one is Fr. Neilson...

I just want you to know that [...] there's a certainty, a joy that's been given to me, not something I made myself, but it's been given to me that cannot be taken away, even in the midst of all of the suffering and pain and whatever it is that I go through [...]Today I'm not in an abandoned building, like a number, that if it didn't exist tomorrow nobody would care. Today I'm a man that's aware of himself because I encountered something to let me know that no matter what, I was created out of love. This love I offer to you because if I didn't know the source of this love I couldn't offer you anything. I prayed for everyone. I'm very happy.

---

[18] https://www.youtube.com/watch?v=MYj5_TPLhdg&t=194s

Frank described the failure of the pain and how he had remembered the billions of people in need of his prayers. This prompted him to reflect:

Either He exists or this is a big scam, but I experienced something here that tells me it's not a big scam. He exists because I made it through all of this stuff, and guess what? I'm still here, I still have my joy, I still have my friends, and I'm still offering. It hasn't been easy, but nothing is impossible with God.

I just want everyone that offered up their prayers for me to know that I too offer every bit of myself for you, and I felt the beauty of the prayers of all the people that prayed for me, and I'm grateful for every breath that I take because I know that my life is part of an embrace, an embrace that cannot be broken by the sorrows of this world.

Frank knew that he was human. "I have anger," he acknowledged, "but I don't have anger towards my brothers."

I just move forward and ask everybody, like Jesus has asked me, to volunteer and walk towards a mystery, the *Mystery, the Mystery of the love that created us all. Forget about our differences. What do we have in common? [...F]eel the love that I'm giving to you now that has been given to me by God.*

He ended the video with expressions of gratitude for everyone – those who prayed for him, me, my poetry, the doctor who had performed the surgery. "Thank you so much and God bless you all."

Climbing Towards Calvary

After the second operation on his heart, Frank was a changed man. Physically he was much weaker and thinner. Before his illness he wore pants with a 38-inch waist. After his diagnosis, his size had decreased to a 36. After his heart surgery, his pants size was 34, then 32, and then 30 inches. He could no longer work, he struggled to eat, and he spent half the day in bed.

The second incision on Frank's chest made the shape of a cross; this was just the first in a series of procedures where blood and water would be drained from his side.

A friend had given me some oil from Saint Joseph's Oratory of Mount Royal in Montreal, Quebec where Saint André Bessette made famous the practice of taking oil from a lamp burning in front of a statue of Saint Joseph and giving it to sick people, telling them to rub in on their body and pray to Saint Joseph for relief. St. André had been a doorman, like Frank. I started rubbing the oil all over Frank's tumors, which were now protruding from his mid-section. As I applied the oil, I prayed the Novena prayer to Saint Joseph which I knew from memory from my days with Mother Teresa's order of nuns, the Missionaries of Charity. I asked for Frank's healing and a happy death. Frank had used to scoff at such practices; now he seemed to bask in them.

Frank loved to relax and watch TV—mostly sports and the Discovery Channel. But even this started to change. He would lie in bed for hours in silence. When I entered the bedroom, I felt as though I were interrupting something. Frank was having long conversations with God. At night, he would grab my hand and pray the Our Father. Many times as we lay in bed together, I would sense a Presence so strong I had the urge to confess my sins out loud. One of those sins was an obsession I'd developed with another man. I couldn't shake it, not even after going to confession. When I asked for forgiveness before God and Frank, Frank looked at me with pity, caressed my head, and said, "My poor wife. She doesn't get any affection from her sick husband." The obsession left me.

As Frank's illness progressed, I realized I could no longer burden him with my pettiness. He often reminded people, "God doesn't care about half of that foolishness that we put ourselves through. He really doesn't. One simple thing: He loves us. If you can keep the fact that God loves you in front of every single thing you do, there's no stopping you."

Jonathan would stop by and have breakfast with Frank at the neighborhood diner, even though Frank couldn't eat much anymore. It began to dawn on Jonathan that he was facing a new trial: "I couldn't lean on Frank so much anymore; I couldn't call him all the time […] I was afraid. […M]y old demonic voices came back: 'How can You take another person from me? How can I walk without this person?'" It would be Frank to help Jonathan take the next step in his journey – the step away from reliance on Frank himself. Jonathan recalls: "Then something new happened. At the School of Community Frank told us, 'You can say all these words, pray all you want, but if this doesn't become experience for you, then it's as if religion is a dream.' He insisted that the way for you to grow was for you to have experience."

The challenges in Jonathan's family and work life intensified, but "for the first time in my life, as a Christian, as an adult man, I decided to test the hypothesis of faith. So I began to internally fight my demons; I challenged them like Frank would challenge me. And I discovered [...] something unbelievable: I was standing. And I couldn't call Frank all the time, but there was a voice inside me now that challenged the demons."

Good Friday was coming up, and Frank was hopeful that Chris Vath would again ask him to carry the cross over the Brooklyn Bridge.

Chris called me and asked, "What do you think?"

"There's no way he's going to make it over the bridge, but he really wants to try."

Chris had an idea. "What if he holds the cross at the beginning, but gives it to someone else before the procession begins? I'll even put a little table in front of him in case he needs to rest it."

I thought it was a great idea. Frank agreed and was very grateful for the compromise.

In preparation for Good Friday, Frank spent the week in intense prayer. One night, I woke up to him praying. Thinking he was talking to me, I said, "What?"

"Shhhh!"

I listened very carefully, but I could only hear him saying things like, "Yes, Lord...."

Suddenly my heart was afflicted with a terrible pain, as if someone had thrust a steel rod into it. I was in so much pain that I couldn't keep quiet. "My heart," I said, "It hurts. It's so cold."

Frank put his hand on my heart and prayed seven Hail Mary*'s*.

When the prayer was finished, I asked him, "Do you realize that you just said seven Hail Mary*'s*?"

"Yes," he said, "And it felt ridiculous!" Frank preferred spontaneous prayer to formal prayer, and he didn't like saying the same prayer over and over again.

"Why did you do it then?"

"Sometimes you're told to do things and you don't ask questions."

I understood immediately that I was being invited to meditate on the Seven Sorrows of Mary. The next day I called Fr. Peter Cameron, and he sent me a Seven Sorrows rosary and a prayer card of Our Lady of Kibeho, who appeared to the visionaries in Rwanda in the early 1980s, before the genocide, and revived the devotion, which was originally revealed to St. Bridget of Sweden in the 14th century. The prayer, and the pain in my heart, which did not go away, became my constant reminder of the gift I was being given.

On Good Friday morning, Frank got dressed up in his suit, which hung on him like a cloak, and together we went to St. James Cathedral in downtown Brooklyn for the Way of the Cross. Timothy Cardinal Dolan, Archbishop of New York, and Bishop Nicholas DiMarzio, Bishop of Brooklyn and Queens were there, as well as Fr. Rich, who was ready to preach along the way. I took my place in the choir, and we sang before a packed church. Frank stood and took the cross, with Thom Black by his side. We sang "Trust in Christ and learn to die./Go to dark Gethsemane." Frank was unsteady but determined. He held the cross over the small table that Chris had set out for him, but never rested it. When it came time for the procession, he handed the cross to another friend in the community, Jon Fromm. It was one of the most heart-wrenching days of my life, to see my husband too sick to walk, with the cross that he loved so much, that he wanted to carry for the entire world. But there was still a Calvary to climb.

My heart was in constant pain, but I never complained. It was an opportunity to share in the work that Christ was doing through Frank for the salvation of the world.

"I'm Always Looking for How God Is Going to Touch My Heart"

That June, Anthony Parranello, the son of our neighbors whom I had been preparing for baptism, was to be baptized. His mother, Janene, asked me to be his godmother, and she said that she wanted Frank to be his godfather. We were both happy and proud, also because Martin would be making his First Communion at the same time. As the day drew closer, Janene decided that she wanted her late husband's Uncle Anthony to be the godfather, instead of Frank. The change of plans crushed him. That night, when we prayed together, Frank asked God to forgive him for being jealous of Eric's Uncle Anthony.

On June 14th, the boys got dressed in white suits, and we all headed to St. Mary Mother of Jesus Church for the Baptism and First Communion celebration. The church was filled with friends and family members. Frank was very sick that day, but he stood by Janene and held her up when she started to collapse from missing Eric, who, for certain, was present and extremely proud.

At the beginning of July, we packed up the car and headed to the Catskills in upstate New York for the CL

Summer Vacation, which was held at Honor's Haven Resort & Spa. Frank was sick and irritable for much of the time and needed to rest in our hotel room. His increased irritability was beginning to take its toll on me. My friend, Tara Sareen, understood that I needed some sort of a break. She offered to take the boys for a couple weeks, which excited them very much, as she had a house full of children and loads of activities planned. Micah and Martin left the vacation and headed to Walpole, Massachusetts, while Frank and I drove back to Brooklyn, and rested for a week before traveling to the Washington, DC area where I was scheduled to give a poetry reading on July 12th. We stayed with my sister, Regina, and her husband Kurt, which was a consolation, especially considering that Regina is a nurse practitioner and always eager to help. Frank's mood had greatly improved, and he was grateful that he could accompany me and show his support. On the night of the reading, he rallied all his strength and was right there, filming and taking pictures. Suzanne Tanzi, who has been my friend since 1988, when we both started attending Communion and Liberation meetings at Saint Patrick's Cathedral in New York City, introduced me to a room full of people, many of whom I already knew. They were extremely gracious and attentive. I read from my Way of the Cross poems, "Fourth Station: Jesus Meets His Mother":

Stay for just a moment longer.
Linger...
But the finger of time
the harshness of circumstance
demand us on.
It is not finished
yet the moment
the perfect moment

picked out of misery
is gone.
A quick glance.
A hand on a shoulder.
We move on.
Is the moment really gone?[19]

During the Q&A, I was asked about my creative process. I answered that I'm not able to write if I'm in conflict with another person. I said that if I'm fighting with my husband, I have to reconcile with him first before the creative juices will flow.

Frank raised his hand while filming and said, "Obviously, she's written a lot of poems, so that means we don't fight that much."

The whole audience erupted into laughter and applause. He continued:

You think when somebody writes a poem, they're sitting in quiet with no one disturbing them; they're able to sit with their thoughts and ponder. But to see what she does, worrying about me being sick all the time, the children constantly harassing her... She has very little sleep, she feeds us, she takes care of all of us, and then she surprises me. At night she'll come in and say, "I wrote this poem today." Where does she have time to write a poem? Now she's got books!

It's an amazing thing when God touches a person; it doesn't follow the normal...process...it gets done somehow or the other. She'll come into the room and read these poems to me. Usually I'm watching the Yankee game, but I listen, and that takes a lot of

---

[19]*Bitterness and Sweet Love*, p. 5.

power to get me from a Yankee game to…poetry, and I'm really amazed at how she can do something so beautiful through all this turmoil that she's going through; I know I'm part of it. And then she'll say, "I'm dedicating this to my husband," and it touches me to my heart…

I know that there's a Presence that has to be present in order for her to be able to express this in the way that she does and how she does. And as your husband, even though I'm biased as heck, I want to thank you.

I was sick. I didn't want to come down to Washington, D.C. I wanted to stay home, but I love my wife so much and her poetry is good. If it wasn't good, then I would've stayed. But I'm very happy that I came to honor a person that could do something like this and can be something to me. I'm looking for something. I'm always looking for…how God or Jesus is going to touch my heart in a special way, and I'm looking far, and I just found out that it's right there, right in front of me. I experienced that tonight. So I just want to thank you for what you do for everyone.

That event was "the perfect moment/picked out of misery."

"I'm Still Living and Offering Everything"

We returned from our trip, and again Frank started having trouble breathing. Francesco Rotatori, our cardiologist friend, came over to the house and listened to Frank's heart and lungs. Frank's heart was strong, but his lungs were filling up with fluid again. The boys were still in Walpole with Anujeet and Tara Sareen and their family, which made it much easier for me to take Frank to the hospital and stay with him. The doctor drained Frank's lungs, but made me understand that the fluid would accumulate again.

At the end of August, our friends in the neighborhood, Chris and Kay Bruno, gave us four tickets to a Brooklyn Cyclones baseball game. Frank was very weak, but wanted to go, so we all got in the car and drove to Coney Island. It was a beautiful, late summer evening. Besides the baseball game, we watched jugglers doing tricks, and clowns spinning hula hoops. The boys were given free baseballs and tee shirts. Frank's sister, Emma, called him during the game, and they had a very heated discussion. She was upset because he wasn't returning her calls, and he was angry because he felt she didn't understand how sick he was. Even before the phone call, Frank was suffering a great deal, but now I could see he was in distress. I asked him if he wanted to go home. He said, no, he wanted the boys to be able to see the end of the game. It was becoming dark, and fireworks started going off from the amusement park next door. Frank smiled as colors exploded in the black sky.

On September 5th, I got a call from one of the Sisters of Life, asking me if I could take food to a mother with several children who was in dire need. Since it was Mother Teresa's feast day, (also Micah's 10th birthday) I did not want to say "no." The boys were in school, and it would be a quick trip, as her apartment building was just a ten-minute car ride away. I had recently gone grocery shopping, so I had a surplus of food. I filled some grocery bags and told Frank that I would be home soon. To my surprise, he got out of bed and said, "I'm coming with you."

"Are you sure?"

"Yes. It's better if you don't go to that neighborhood by yourself."

When we got to the woman's apartment building, I texted her, and her oldest son came downstairs and met us. Frank told me to stay in the car. He gave the young man two bags and he took two bags himself, and followed the woman's son into the building. "You're walking too fast, man," Frank said. "I'm a stage four cancer patient."

I prayed to Mother Teresa the whole time I was in the car waiting. I was afraid that Frank would collapse with the grocery bags, trying to keep up. The woman we were helping was the same woman Frank had prayed and offered for, so that she would not abort her youngest child. She was on the fence for a long time, but finally decided to have the baby. She and the father were both very happy with their newborn daughter.

When Frank came out of the building, I rejoiced. He sat in the car out of breath and somewhat surprised that the woman did not even come to the door to say "thank you." Still, he was happy that God had given him the strength to help her.

Frank was admitted to the hospital on two separate occasions that September. Both times he was struggling to breathe because his lungs were full of fluid. The second crisis was more dramatic than the first because I had to call the ambulance in the middle of the night, and my sister Susan had to come and stay with the boys. Thank God they never woke up to all the commotion.

The ambulance looked like something stolen from the Beverly Hillbillies. The driver kept asking Frank questions while he was struggling to breathe. I begged them to take us to Maimonides Hospital, where Dr. Abrol was, but they insisted on Coney Island Hospital because it was the closest. We had no choice but to go there. The emergency room was empty, with just a couple of drunk men lying on cots. The staff seemed nonchalant as Frank fought for every breath. One nurse dropped a vial on the floor and, instead of picking it up, kicked it under the bed. I wanted to get out of there as soon as possible. The hospital finally got an ambulance to transfer Frank to Maimonides, where he once again waited on a bed in a curtained off section of the ER, with other people in crisis all around him. Fortunately, I had Frank's pain medication in my purse, so he did not have to wait for a doctor's approval for a nurse to parcel out pain pills. At one point there was a lot of movement to the left of us. Frank and I could both sense that the medical staff was working to save someone's life. We started praying. After a couple minutes, the effort ceased, and we saw family members hugging and crying. Frank was deeply touched that he had been privileged to assist, with his prayers and suffering, this stranger who was making the journey home. It wasn't long before Dr. Abrol was at his side, once again arranging to have Frank's lungs drained.

Frank's intense suffering during these days corresponded with the anguish of our nation. On August 9, 2014, in Ferguson, MO, a white police officer, Darren Wilson fatally shot an 18-year-old black man, Michael Brown, causing terrible riots to break out. When people asked Frank for his opinion about the situation, he never wanted to comment, perhaps because the problem of racism was too painful for him, and he felt that people who hadn't experienced it couldn't really understand, and their misunderstanding would only make it more painful. Or maybe it was because he felt that talking about it wouldn't do anything to change it. There was also a stubbornness in Frank, a refusal to be the spokesperson for any cause no matter how noble or well-intended. "I'm Frank," he would say. By personality, Frank had always grabbed ahold of things that he felt were useful or positive for his life, and didn't give his time to negative things. He said many times, "We've been given many more good things, than bad." Once he told me, "If good weren't stronger than evil, we would've destroyed each other a long time ago." Yet Frank was far from passive. After he had his lungs drained, I filmed *Frank Speak 8* as he lay in his hospital bed waiting for tests. I am certain that Ferguson was on his mind and in his heart when he made this video.

2014-09-29 Frank Speak 8[20]

---

[20] https://www.youtube.com/watch?v=BZF4pNGn4QU&t=6s

It's been a long time since I've been able to check in with everyone. I'm here in the hospital, thanks be to God. I'm still hanging on. It was 2 years, 4 months ago when I was told that I had 6 months to live, but I'm still here because my life is in the hands of something much greater than myself. I've learned through this experience that my suffering, my sins, have a meaning because I can offer them up for you, for my fellow man, and for world peace. This isn't something that you have to intellectualize; it's something that you experience—something that makes suffering have a sweetness to it. I know you may say that it's ridiculous. How could suffering have a sweetness to it? But it does because it points you back to why you were created in the first place...and what love it took to create you that will permeate all the diversity and adversity that you have to go through just to live. [...]

Who says we have to go out with guns and try to dominate and fight for peace in that way? I suggest that the power of prayer, when it comes from your heart...when it really shows the love that's been given to you, can be transferred in this world in a way that you don't decide who God blesses, you just ask God to bless who he knows needs these blessings. It makes you so important because the importance of the man isn't decided by what the man thinks; it's decided by a loving, beautiful God, whose benevolence and love is greater than anything we know.

I ask you to keep your strength up, anyone that's suffering like I am...Together we can overcome this world problem because we pray, we offer. We can't be like our enemy, but we can even pray for our enemy. I thank you. Don't be too judgmental on the next man; start by looking at yourself...and ask your own heart what do you really feel about the creation that God created and said that it was good? Where is that goodness now? I thank you, in Jesus Christ's Holy Name.

As Frank was in and out of the hospital, struggling to breathe, so was our dear friend, Msgr. Lorenzo Albacete. He had been sick for some time, and it seemed he was nearing his final days.

On October 7th, Frank was again admitted to the hospital to have his lungs drained, but this time he was so traumatized by the experience of not being able to breathe that we felt we needed a better solution. The medical staff proposed we have oxygen delivered to our house. This seemed to help. From that point on, Frank did not go anywhere without his oxygen tank.

Frank was also traumatized by the callous indifference of some of the hospital staff. While he was waiting to get tests done, a young staff member, who was supposed to be taking care of him, was showing pictures from her phone to another staff member, and they were laughing loudly, while Frank lay on the cot, shivering and in pain. He came back to his hospital room in tears.

"That Monsignor Is a Funny Dude"

We knew that Msgr. Albacete was very close to death, and in spite of the fact that Frank had recently been released from the hospital, he felt a great urgency to make the trip to Westchester Medical Center in Valhalla, New York, to see his dear friend. I, too, was worried that we wouldn't get there in time. Our friend, Olivetta, was helping to coordinate visits, and she said that Monsignor would love to see us. We made the trip on October 15th, Fr. Giussani's birthday, and asked for his intercession for a happy meeting. It was cold and rainy that day. I helped Frank down the steps of our apartment with his oxygen tank, and we drove for over an hour. When we arrived, I was so nervous, I started moving very quickly, frustrating Frank, who was wheeling his oxygen tank behind me. Olivetta met us in the waiting room and led us to the unit where Monsignor was. Again, I ran ahead of Frank. When I entered the unit, I looked in all the rooms, but did not see him. "Where is Msgr. Albacete?" I asked, frantically, to no one in particular.

A nurse heard me and said, "He's right there." She pointed at someone who looked nothing like him.

I approached Monsignor's bed. He was very swollen, and so clean he seemed to sparkle. He looked at me and asked, "How are you?"

"Monsignor, Frank is dying!" I blurted out, surprising myself. I quickly calmed down as I saw Frank coming into the room.

Frank went to the other side of Monsignor's bed, and broke down in tears. "Lord, have mercy on this man! Have mercy on Your servant, Lorenzo, who means so much to me!"

Frank held Monsignor's right hand, and I, his left. We prayed an Our Father and a Hail Mary together. Frank continued in spontaneous prayer and then became silent, pursed his lips and started nodding his head. We stood in silence for a few more minutes, and then Frank looked up at me and said, "Okay, let's go."

It seemed like a very quick visit, but I imagined Frank needed to get off his feet, and besides, we had to be home on time for me to pick the boys up from school.

On the drive home, Frank said, "Monsignor told me that I need to go to confession." I wanted to say, "But he didn't say anything to you," but at this point, I knew better.

"I did something real foul when I was a kid, and I need to confess it. I'd tell you what it is, but I don't think you could handle it."

"I don't want to know!" I said, and I meant it. "I'll call St. Mary's and ask Msgr. Vaccari if he can come over to the house; you can tell him."

As soon as we got home, and Frank was settled in his bed, I phoned our pastor, Msgr. Andrew Vaccari, and he came immediately.

When I announced his arrival, Frank said to me, "You didn't waste any time."

"We've been married eleven years," I told him, "you should know by now that there are certain things your wife doesn't play around with."

Msgr. Lorenzo Albacete passed away nine days later, on October 24, 2014. His last words, which came from his child-like heart and passed through his ever-playful lips were, "You see, Jesus always comes. He wants to be with us."

Frank and I couldn't do enough to honor this man. I made a slideshow, and also wrote a poem:

"Alas"

Msgr. Lorenzo Albacete
the anti-Pharisee.
Outside the cup is chipped
cracked
caked with crumbs.
The inside
seen by only One.
But we can glimpse
through
pure blue
brilliance
if we dare
to stare
into that sea—
Alas,
the crash—
Humanity!

Msgr. Albacete's body was placed in the middle aisle near the altar of St. Mary's Church on the Lower East Side of Manhattan for the viewing. A swarm of older women from the parish surrounded his coffin and were touching him. I entered the circle, and quickly and covertly plucked a single white hair from his head. When I came home and told Frank what I had done, he went into the bathroom, shaved his head and put all his hair in a Ziploc bag. He handed it to me, and said, "There, is that enough for you?"

At the funeral Mass, which was celebrated by Monsignor's good friend, Sean Cardinal O'Malley, Archbishop of Boston, Frank cried so hard that his oxygen tube became clogged, and he could barely breathe. At the end of Mass, as the pall bearers were getting ready to wheel his coffin down the aisles, one of the priests on the altar shouted, "L O R E N Z O!" Frank nearly doubled over, but he regained his composure enough to follow the coffin out to the street in front of the church where a mariachi band was playing. Frank started to dance.

That night, I was again wakened from sleep to find Frank having a conversation.

"What?", I said, thinking he was talking to me.

"Shhhhhh."

The conversation went on for a while and, when it ended, Frank laughed and said, "That Monsignor is a funny dude."

"You were talking with him?"

"Yes, and he said 'You're missing out on a big party up here.' And then he said, 'Tell Rita not to worry about anything, and tell Rita that everything we believe about God is true.'"

The next day, Frank sat at the kitchen table in his bathrobe, and I filmed him as he paid tribute to one of the most important men in his life, who had "traveled his road, even till the end, [in a way that] really touched my heart." "His humor, his quickness of thought and intelligence comes with him and goes with him," Frank said, "but yet he leaves a sign of the Father, the Son and Holy Spirit for all of us to benefit from." Frank went on to give details about the impact his relationship with Albacete had had on him:

2014-10-29 Frank Speak 9 [21]

[...]

I just want to tell you a little bit about him, though. [...] You'd think that, when you'd see the two of us sitting down, it was all this real serious conversation, but we would laugh together over the most trivial subjects! Yet I would come prepared for the most serious subjects. For instance, I went to the Memores Domini *house[, where we were invited for Easter dinner,] one time, and I called him just to see what he needed.*

"Hello, Frank."

"What's going on, Monsignor?"

"I've told you many times, my name is Lorenzo."

"Yes, Lorenzo." (You know, a guy of such high esteem... You want to meet him on the level that your mind perceives, so I always called him Monsignor, and apparently he wanted something a little bit closer, more intimate than that... So I said:)

"What can I get you?"

"Well, we could start with some fried chicken."

"Monsignor, I can't bring fried chicken into the Memores *house. You've gotta be kidding me."*

"No, I'm not kidding."

---

[21] https://www.youtube.com/watch?v=vkoFgNzme0E&t=5s

"Are you sure this isn't gonna be disrespectful?"

"I don't care."

"How am I supposed to get this into the house?"

"You forgot, Frank, I know everything about you. If anyone could do it, you could definitely smuggle chicken into the Memores *house."*

Frank said that he would try, but then decided against it. Fried chicken was strictly blacklisted due to Monsignor's health, and Frank wanted him to live. Unable to tolerate the prospect of being at fault for losing Albacete, he opted not to smuggle in the chicken.

So no, I didn't try to get the chicken in, and the first thing he asked me when we came was, "Can we talk in private?"

I knew he was gonna ask me. "Where is it?"

"Where's what?"

"The chicken."

"If I had brought you this chicken, how are you going to tell all these people that I brought you this fried chicken?

"I'll tell them the chicken made me do it."

[...Even now that his physical boundaries have been broken, I still hear him asking for chicken, I still see him having a great party, wherever he is. He doesn't have to worry about chicken anymore, and he's reaching out to those that he loves, inviting them to join this party with him. There are no more barriers

of weight, and joy is in abundance where he is. I know you won't believe me, but he told me himself.

I give the highest honor to this man, to Monsignor...to Lorenzo, I'm sorry, Lorenzo. There are not many people that you'll come across in your life that will, without even opening their mouths, point you directly to God. He's one of them, [...] and I'm grateful for every second that I spent with Lorenzo [...].

Then Frank recalled a chapter from our engagement, the first time he'd met Monsignor:

I was ready to fight against the policies of different religious traditions, so my wife brought me to him. I turned the corner expecting to have some stiff priest, ready to give me all the rules and regulations. And instead, there's this man [Frank described his stature as "Alfred Hitchcock"], sitting in the chair, cigarette in his mouth. He turns to me and he says, 'How are you doing, Frank?' And it washed away all of the fight in me just for him to talk to me on a personal level. He changed me with just a couple of words. He pointed out things to me in words that no one would have actually known what was in my heart, as if he knew me since I was a child. And talk about somebody changing you, and talk about someone giving you another chance in life—it was him.

It's 11 or 12 years down the line, and I myself am sick, but I'm still with the wife that he pointed me to and told me during my wedding ceremony, "Frank, if you want to, you can still run out the church before putting the ring on Rita." And I said, "No." I was certain, and I'm very grateful for the opportunity for conversion that I received, and it wasn't something real big and fantastic and elaborate at that moment. It was a gesture from a man that showed me the love of God with just one or two little words, and now I'm so emotional about it because he's gone, but yet again he's not. He will stick with us through thick and thin, and his hand is always reaching out, asking us to join the party.

The days ahead were even more intense. I kept thinking about Monsignor's words to Frank, "Tell Rita not to worry about anything."

Though Frank was getting sicker and sicker, this didn't change the relentless running around we had to do. Tests had to be done, and the results hand delivered. Trips to the oncologist were particularly difficult. I had to drop Frank off in front of the hospital with his oxygen tank, and then look for parking, unless I decided to spend an exorbitant amount of money paying for a space in a garage. The best solution was finding a spot at a parking meter, though this still posed difficulties:

"Buying Time"

The need to appease the parking meter breaks me from my husband's side.
This city seems cold and calculating, extracting quarters,
but counting the cost? Unqualified.

During this period of great suffering, Frank and I were making new friends. A group of people in CL in Spain learned about Frank through an article in a magazine put out by CL, *Traces*. They asked if we would be willing to Skype with them. We also Skyped with an American family stationed in the army in Germany, the Bucalos, and, in spite of the distance, became very close friends.

Frank spent that Thanksgiving in the hospital. Once again his lungs were filling up with fluid and he was struggling to breathe. The boys were with my mother, having dinner at our friends', the Ronans. I was alone with Frank. He was sleeping, and I was trying to rest, but couldn't because of all the heart monitors' nonstop dinging on the floor. I kept seeing the Grinch, with drumsticks beating each side of his head, saying, "Noise, noise, noise, noise." I took out my *Magnificat* magazine and started reading, hoping it would help.

"The night is far advanced. The day is near," I read (from Romans 13:12). Yes, I thought, the darkness seems victorious, growing darker, gaining strength. But darkness is on a time clock. Its power runs out. The darker the darkness, the closer the day! Day is the winner. Day has the last say. Darkness's defeat is inevitable. Its power is finite; it is no contender for the day. Evil is anxious. It knows it's bound for defeat. That's why it grabs at things indiscriminately, has no loyalty, takes whatever it can, never builds. It hates its finiteness, but can't do anything about it. Its existence is hatred of what it can never be, so its desire is to ruin what it envies. There was a battle raging, and I was on the front lines. I sat and wrote in the margins of my *Magnificat*:

Where night is far advanced,
destruction has its dance.
It shakes and quivers
joints, bends back-
wards into
black.
The dance advances on
to break the dark with dawn at last.

213

Still, Frank's final stay in Maimonides Medical Heart and Vascular Center was a sad one. I could tell from the staff's attitude that they didn't see any hope for his recovery. Frank wanted to start his chemotherapy again, but I was concerned that he wasn't strong enough. I spoke with the nurse practitioner on the floor, and she said, "If he wants it, give it to him." I spoke with Renzo Canetta, our cancer researcher friend who'd been guiding us since Frank's diagnosis, and he didn't think it was a good idea. I asked Renzo to speak with the nurse practitioner, and she again affirmed Frank's desire to continue his cancer treatment.

"I Am a Changed Man"

After finishing his chemotherapy, Frank began fading very quickly. I knew that he wanted to die at home, but I did not know how to take care of him. I called my sister, Regina, who was a geriatric nurse practitioner, and she told me to call Calvary Hospital and get a hospice nurse and nurse's aide to come to the house. She drove up from Fairfax, Virginia and helped me get the bedroom in order. We put a big table by the bed and stacked it with medical supplies. We also had hand rails installed in the bathroom. The hospice nurse ordered a bedside commode and a shower chair.

Frank's firstborn, Marshall, came over and crawled right into bed with his father. Marshall's mother, Bobbie Ann, called and told me, "I have two best friends, and Frankie is one of them."

I phoned his daughter Wendi in Tennessee and told her the end was near. She broke down and cried, and told me she would try and come and see her father as soon as possible.

Fr. Paul Anel, a priest from Heart's Home, a Catholic faith community that lives among the poor, came to visit. Frank and I would often give witnesses at Heart's Home volunteer training sessions. When he saw Fr. Paul at his bedside, Frank smiled, and with what little strength he had, spoke about the Virgin Mary: "She truly is a mother; she truly is a mother."

Tiffiny came, despite her physical challenges, and brought a special pillow which helped Frank to sit up when he had to try to eat, drink or take his medication. She told me that she asked Jesus if she could have all of Frank's suffering. When I told Frank, he said, "That's not what God wants."

The boys stopped going into the bedroom. It was becoming too traumatic for them to watch their father die. I allowed them to listen to music on their computers or play video games, knowing they needed the distraction. My mother was a big help. As long as she was around, I didn't have to worry about cooking, cleaning or tending to the boys.

After just a few days at home, Frank was starting to lose consciousness. I called the Sisters of Life and begged for prayers. Mother Agnes called me back and left a message on the answering machine. "Don't worry, Rita. Ninety nun are praying." After I listened to the message, I went into the bedroom. Regina was trying to sit Frank up to take his pain medication. I went to the other side of the bed to assist. It was very difficult, since he was unresponsive. "Frank!" I said, "Ninety nuns are praying for you!"

Suddenly he opened his eyes. He looked at me and Regina sliding him around on the under pad.

"What are you all trying to do?"

"Frank, we're trying to sit you up so you can take your medicine," I said.

"Well, why didn't you just say so?" He placed his hands near his hips and hiked himself up. Then he mumbled, "Ninety nuns praying, and you all can't do a simple thing."

It was truly miraculous! Frank had revived. On December 5th, he got out of bed and walked to the living room, where he sat on the couch and made *Frank Speak 10*, thanking all those who had prayed him back to life, and praising the beauty and the "caress" of God. More than in any of the previous videos, the contrast between Frank's physical state and his joy was on display. Unable to hold his head up, it is propped against the back of the couch, and looks small and frail in the middle of the shot. His eyes seem to fall shut several times as he's speaking, as if he lacks the strength even to keep them open. In the beginning we hear him make an effort to speak in normal tones, but this fails, and the voice that speaks the words below is thin and high-pitched, no longer recognizable. But the contents testify to a man who was more alive than ever before, and who was still actively living the revolution of his relationship with God: "a changed man," as he puts it.

2014-12-05 Frank Speak 10[22]

I just want to thank everybody for their prayers [...]. I've gone through some very hard times recently, almost to the point where we all thought that I would not be here today to even do this video, but I'm grateful. A changed man. A man that's learned to depend upon the caress of God.

This is no joke, my friends. I thought that God was getting ready to call me home. [...I]t came down to the last couple of minutes, when I felt the embrace of God, and it was such a beautiful embrace, but he also told me it's not time for me to go anywhere.

He's kept me, and I'm so grateful, and I know now that I'm a changed man, a blessed man that is willing to share everything that's happened to him with you.

So if you feel like things are just so bad that you can't handle them, try God. He never forgets, He's always forgiving and loving, and He can't wait to help you.

My friends, I love you all very much. I can't wait to see you.

Every new day is another day that we can be grateful for the love of God.

Thank you very much.

There was a sense of triumph in the house. Frank had once again escaped death. He wanted to keep his appointment with the oncologist and ask for another round of chemo. I wanted to skip the appointment and allow him to regain some more strength. He insisted on going. I couldn't imagine how I was going to get him down the apartment steps. I told Frank I would only take him if I had help. He agreed. I asked our neighbor, Chris Bruno, and he was more than happy to lend a hand. He came and helped Frank down the steps while I took the oxygen tank. Chris drove us to Manhattan and dropped us off at the entrance to Mount Sinai at Union Square. It was a great relief not to have to worry about parking the car. Still I was very nervous. I had to get Frank a wheelchair. When I found one, he sat down, but the tube from his oxygen tank got tangled in the wheel. It took a while for me to figure out how to untangle it. When we finally reached our destination, Frank stood up and approached the reception desk. The staff was very familiar with Frank, and they loved him. He was always smiling and encouraging the other patients. They were shocked to see him so frail and thin. When we entered Dr. Kozuch's office, the nurse practitioner, Priscilla Kim, looked at Frank, and her eyes filled with tears. "I'm so sorry," she said. And she repeated, "I mean it; I'm really sorry."

Dr. Kozuch came into the room. "What can I do for you, Frank?"

"I want to continue my treatment."

"I can't give it to you, buddy," Dr. Kozuch said.

Frank sat on the end of the examination table, pursed his lips, and nodded his head.

Dr. Kozuch looked at Priscilla. "I think he could use a Vitamin D shot."

She ordered the shot, and we went to the chemo suite for a shot of Vitamin D.

Christmas was coming, and I hadn't bought a single gift. I had to get something for the boys. My sister, Regina, had gone back to Virginia, and my mother wouldn't allow me to leave her alone with Frank, since she feared he would have a crisis on her watch. I had to wait for the nurse's aide to come. She was a very young Hispanic woman who was supposedly trained in hospice care. I hadn't been gone fifteen minutes, when she called me on my cell phone. "He wants his dungarees."

"Ok. You can give them to him."

She hesitated. "What are they?"

I had to laugh. "They're blue jeans."

A half hour later, she called me again. "He can't breathe."

The hospice nurse had given us a sealed box that contained a morphine shot. I told her to give it to him. She seemed reluctant.

"Call Calvary," I told her, "and they'll walk you through it."

I rushed home and found Frank sitting on the bed with just his jeans on, struggling to breathe. She had given him the morphine shot, which was starting to help. My mother was in the kitchen, looking very upset. "He didn't want me to interfere," she said.

Later that day, I asked Frank if he would consider in-patient hospice care.

"What is it?"

I explained that, instead of having the nurses come to him, he would go to them, and if he had a breathing crisis, he would already be in a place where a whole team of medical staff would know exactly what to do. But Calvary Hospital in Brooklyn had only twenty-five beds, so if he wanted to go, we would have to put his name on a waiting list.

"Ok," he said.

"It's Not Hard to Love God"

On December 21st, Frank made another video as he lay in bed. He seemed like he was at the threshold of another world. Despite his weakness, his eyes were luminous, and he could not keep a smile from his lips as he described the love he was experiencing. He even broke into a grin as he made a joking reference to "Miller time," a line from a beer commercial that used the Miller beer brand to refer to the greatest moments in life.

2014-12-21 Frank Speak 11[23]

Another day given to us by the Lord, a day to ponder the beauty of our love. It's really interesting how God just grasps us and leads us on a path that is so beautiful that it's almost beyond our comprehension.

I've learned to love at a rate that is so high that I can barely comprehend it. The only thing that allows me to comprehend is when I look at you, I look at my wife, I look at my children, I look at my family.

---

[23] https://www.youtube.com/watch?v=vYclZLRDgWY&t=8s

Yes, things have not gone the greatest in my life, but they've gone great; they've gone beautiful. And, just so that you know, God is merciful and he loves us beyond anything we can imagine.

I want to say one thing, and I say it from the depth of my heart: I would have never imagined that God himself would be inside myself to a point...the love that he's allowed me to see. It's almost like Moses being allowed to walk across the Red Sea. And I'm grateful, very grateful to have you, and to have such friends that allow me to have someone to hold on to, to embrace during these times.

It's morning time now. I don't know what time it is, but I tell you what, any time with God is Miller time because He allows me to see myself, and be myself, and look at myself in a way that God wants me to see myself.

Oh God, oh God, I thank You for all of these benefits and prayers that You've given me, and I just bless You because You bless me. Thank You, thank You, thank You.

It's not hard to love God. As a matter of fact, it's very easy.

Thank you once again, my friends. As I speak to you, my heart shakes, the world quakes at just the sound of Your voice. Just to know that at one point in Your life, You took out a space and said, "Frank, I love you."

In the Holy Name of Jesus, Amen.

Immediately after I posted the video, I got a call from Italy. It was Fr. Vincent Nagle, the priest who had asked Frank for his blessing after Frank's witness in Pittsburgh a little over a year before. Fr. Vincent, who had been a hospital chaplain, knew the end was near. Frank told him that he wanted to die at home.

Later that day, Wendi came to visit, along with Marshall and Marshall's cousin Leontes. Frank was already exhausted by evening time, but he rallied for pictures with all four of his children. Micah and Martin were extremely happy to be with their older brother and sister, and they enjoyed playing piano with Leontes. The hospice nurse told us that Frank would probably not make it to Christmas.

"I Will Not Leave This World Hating My Wife"

On December 23rd, Frank surprised everyone. He woke up feeling better than he had in a long time. He was able to eat, walk around the house, and make a few phone calls to family and friends. He told Rachel Oberman, "I think I'm going to get the miracle we've been praying for." It was the worst possible day to get a call from Calvary Hospital saying that they had a bed for him. I had no idea how I would break the news, but was warned that if we turned them down, they'd never offer us a bed again. So I accepted. The ambulance was on its way.

"Frank, remember how you put your name on a wait list for Calvary Hospital?" I asked timidly.

"No," he said, "What are you talking about?"

When I tried to explain, he became very upset. "You're trying to put me out of my own home!"

My mother was in the kitchen crying.

"Frank, if you really don't want to go," I told him, "I'll call Calvary right now and tell them not to come."

My mother was in the background, shaking her head, mouthing, "No, no, no."

I was praying to God for help when the phone rang. It was my brother-in-law, Ken. "How's Frank today?"

"He's upset with me," I said, and explained what was going on.

"Let me talk to him," Ken said.

I put Ken on speaker phone. "Frank, you have to go to Calvary. Your wife can't take care of you anymore. You have to do it for Rita."

I was shocked by Ken's directness. I could never have said what he said.

Frank thought for a moment. Then he simply said, "Okay."

No sooner had I hung up the phone than the ambulance driver was at the door. Two men came upstairs with a chair that had a strap on it.

"What does he need to bring?" I asked.

"Nothing." They carried Frank onto the chair and strapped him in. "He's good to go."

Frank looked all around the bedroom as they lifted the chair and carried him away. It was rainy and cold outside. I held an umbrella over Frank's head before they put him into the ambulance. Our downstairs neighbor, Andrew, was watching. "Good bye, Frank Simmonds," he called out with a starkness that seemed to echo.

I told Frank that I would follow in the car. I ran upstairs, where my mother was still crying in the kitchen. "Poor Frank. That was so hard for him." Then she became very authoritative, "I don't care what I tell you when I get sick. I'm telling you right now. Put me in hospice!"

I called Rachel Oberman, our good friend from the neighborhood where the health clinic was, and told her Frank was on his way to Calvary. She was shocked. "I just spoke with him this morning and he sounded great."

I asked her if she could meet me there, and she agreed.

When I got to Calvary, I was amazed by the calm and beauty of the place. It was decorated with lights and

Christmas trees, and the staff was receptive, kind and accommodating. Frank had his own room with a big window, and it was very clean. But he was not happy. A volunteer came by wheeling a refreshment cart and asked me if I wanted something to drink.

"Do you have anything strong?" I asked.

"Would you like a glass of wine?"

"You have wine?" I was amazed.

He poured me a cold glass of white wine, and I sat and drank while Frank glared at me. Rachel came, and I left to talk with the social worker. "In eleven years of marriage, my husband has never looked at me with the disdain he has now," I told her, and started to cry.

The social worker explained that it's very common. He just needs time, she said, and offered to try to talk to him. I was open to any kind of improvement. She went into Frank's room and came out in ten minutes. "Rita, your husband has something he wants to tell you."

I went into his room. He was sitting up in bed, so regal and dignified that I was overwhelmed by the thought that he looked like a proud African king on a throne.

"Frank," the social worker said, "Tell Rita what you told me."

He made this pronouncement: "I will not leave this world hating my wife."

Frank was not going to fake it. He was still angry.

The next day, he was still somewhat cool towards me, but early on Christmas morning, I called him and his voice was completely different. "I had trouble breathing last night. Thank God I was here."

"It's Not as Bad as it Looks"

After the initial adjustment, Frank became the most magnanimous dying man Calvary Hospital had ever seen. On the day after Christmas, Fr. Rich Veras came and celebrated Mass in the community room. All of our friends and family members were invited. The room was packed. The hospital staff helped to get Frank out of bed and into a wheelchair. It was quite a job since he was hooked up to an IV, a catheter and an oxygen tank.

During Mass, Fr. Rich spoke about St. Stephen, and explained that the Church celebrates the first Christian martyr the day after Christmas because Christmas celebrates the day God became a frail human being, which is God's martyrdom.

At the end of Mass, Frank, in all his frailty, had the desire to speak:

I am grateful for everything I have been given. I wouldn't change a thing.

Everyone in this room is here for a reason.

I have talked the talk; now it's time to walk the walk. But I'm not afraid because I know I don't walk alone.

Then my mother shouted out: "Frank, you have a heart as big as the whole world!"

He responded:

God did that for me, and he can do that for you, too. He can do that for every person in this room. I have been given a mission to love everyone, and I give that mission now to every person in this room. You can love everyone that you meet. Not by carrying a Giussani sign, but by being that sign of God's love.

Then he asked us not to pity him. "It's not as bad as it looks." And everyone laughed because he did look pretty bad.

After Mass, the hospital staff put him back in bed, but there were people that he wanted to see. He asked me to go and get them. I was moved by the people he asked for – they were not the friends he communicated with often, but people he cared about, or who had been kind to him, and he wanted to be sure to see them and express his love and gratitude.

Bobby Tannenhauser made sure that Frank received all his Christmas cards, with uplifting messages and generous tips from the residents of Ruxon Towers, who missed their gregarious doorman.

Calvary seemed more like Bethlehem, such was the draw of this man, immobile in a bed. So many people came, as though following a star.

"Time for the Treasuring"

It was Bethlehem.
The star settled over his bed,
became larger and larger,
filled his eyes.
Earl came in the early hours of the morning,
Anthony came quietly, in the middle of the night.
Maureen came after work.
Raquel came and drew pictures of his thinning face
and growing hair.
Jonathan came and sat and stood and paced.
Susan came and released her tears.
David came and prayed while he slept.
Ann came to watch and hear.
Peter came; they laughed and embraced.
Justin came with his fiancé.
Sofi came with her fiancé.
Simo and Joe came in sorrow and reverence.
Patricia came, messaged his hands and soothed his
skin.
Cas and Valentina came and sang, as did Virginio
and Ernesto, Barbara and Bev.
Theresa came with a scapular.
Althea came with her friends.
Paul came and told jokes.
Ewa and Eric came for help.

Fr. Solanus came and anointed his head.
Bobby Ann came and kissed his face.
Marshall came and saw the Seahawks win.
Duane came with a Yankee cap.
Emma came and lost her specs.
Alfred came and took it all in.
Wendi came and sat on his bed.
Doreen came with family and gifts.
John and Connie came and listened to him.
Ted came to celebrate.
Rachel came and stayed when I had to leave.
Regina came and watched him breathe.
Naomi and Ken came as if they'd never left.
Maryann came and wept at the foot of his bed.
Sebby came and wanted to stay the night.
John Touhey came and left with joy.
Riro came and heard him cry out.
Renzo came full of hope.
Sr. Regine came and smiled.
Chris Vath came and brought comfort.
Michael and Olga came and were comforted.
Micah and Martin came and ate ice cream.
*Mom came and talked and ate and chased our boys
around the place.*
Derrick came right off the plane.
Fr. Peter came before his flight.
Tiffiny and Peggy came via speaker phone.
Francesco came and listened to his heart and lungs.
Fr. Joe came and didn't want to leave.
Msgr. Vaccari came and forgave his sins.
Fr. Jose came and asked about Ferguson.
Fr. Rich came and preached about St Stephen.
*Frank addressed his people and gave them their
mission.*

When the angels came and filled the room with peace,
I knew it was the time for treasuring.

Chris Bacich wrote in CL's magazine, *Traces*, "When Frank speaks, when he looks at you, it is with the eyes of a child. And in front of them, I become a shepherd, gazing in wonder that such a child should be, stunned to silence that God has taken human flesh and called me to witness it."

On New Year's Eve, several friends gathered around Frank's bed to ring in 2015. Our friend, Ted Oberman, would later write about that evening:

A group of us spent the hours approaching midnight with Frank and Rita Simmonds at the hospice... The evening slipped by doing what we would do most other New Year's. Everyone had brought some food or drink, and we passed the time talking, and then singing. Considering the incredible amount of musicality in the room, it was surprising how many verses to songs we forgot, though we did manage our way through Homeward Bound *and* Falling in Love with You, *to name a few. Frank was quiet most of the evening, his breath labored, and at certain points we thought that this might be his last night. Rita did rouse him a few times, and seeing us he would draw the words "my friends" from within...In spite of his pain, Frank was truly a witness to faith, and present in life amid his suffering...Serenading our brother, we saw Frank, and all the good memories of him, placed against a future without his physical presence. More than that though, we saw that evening how suffering and pain could not diminish in Frank the sweet expectation of the world to come.*

"It's Not the End that's Coming; It's the Beginning"

On New Year's Day, Janene and Anthony came and stayed for Mass. I asked the hospice chaplain if he would offer the Mass for Eric, who had died one year before. He agreed. Janene wept through the whole liturgy, but thanked me profusely.

Frank always took care to express his gratitude for the care he received. Like with that too-small pair of shoes, years ago, he took nothing for granted. One of Frank's favorite doctors from the union health clinic, Dr. Anton Rostovsky, worked at Calvary on weekends. Frank thought it was a tremendous gift to have the opportunity to express his gratitude to a man who had gone out of his way to make sure Frank received the proper treatment under very challenging circumstances. He was also visited by another doctor from the clinic, Dr. Mary Chang, who fought hard to coordinate Frank's complicated treatment.

There was a young orderly, Denis, who always made sure that Frank was clean and comfortable. One day Frank told him, "There is no man in this hospital as great as you." I later learned that Denis had not lived long after we knew him.

He had other messages he wished to get across, as well. Once, Frank asked me to go and get the medical director, Dr. Irina Makarevich. He told her how grateful he was for the care he was being given, yet advised her to pray very hard "because the devil is at the door, trying to get in." Dr. Makarevich later told me, "When the dying tell you things, it's important to listen."

Often Frank would ask me to get a pen and paper, and dictate to me. Some of the contents indicate how much his experience had changed the views he held when we met. He spoke a lot about the importance of the weekly Communion and Liberation meetings, the School of Community. He took care to say that the rules of the Church are beneficial. "If you can, get them from Fr. Rich because he was given the authority to deal with things like this." He said that, "God wants our obedience. He wants us to totally trust Him, and if you think you've heard it before, you're wrong, because if you did hear it and accept it, I wouldn't be here to tell you." He stressed the importance of not playing games, but listening to God, and explained that God speaks to us in reality, which is "a series of questions asking you how much you really believe your life is worth, not only to you, but to God."

He mentioned how often we miss the message that God is trying to communicate, and spoke about vocation: "When God calls you…He means business. He means that He's going to take your life and allow you to see what's been there the whole time: His love for you, the love that created you." He talked about God's sovereignty. "God reigns supreme. If He could take my heart and change it, He can change yours."

He stressed that, "this world needs loyalty, devotion. It doesn't need people running from problems." He referenced Pope Francis' message, that we need to move forward, "and stop walking in fear of everything. Walk with your head up high, no matter what happens, because what we have can neither be bought, broken or stolen." But, he warned, "woe to the person who changes the road that God has laid out for us."

At times, his words took on a prophetic tone. "It's not the end that's coming; it's the beginning… The beginning of a conversion, a new life – one that's being pushed along by Christ." He added that, whoever felt those words, God would need them next.

He spoke about his confidence in Christ: "He's not worried about me. I'm His." And he was certain that, "This drama has a happy ending" from which "there's no turning back."

He said that the Lord was going to allow him to look at everyone who'd been a part of his journey, and show them something they hadn't seen yet: "a special touch from God."

One day he predicted that God was going to allow him to see women in a different light, and added, "Women are the most beautiful thing that can happen to a man." This one struck me as particularly personal because, since the betrayal Frank had experienced with his mother's departure, he had always had difficulty trusting women.

There were times when Frank felt so weak that he could barely speak. On one such day, he asked me to write down a name, Joni Walaski, the friend from the business loan company who used to give him Yankee tickets, and who hadn't spoken to him since their argument years earlier. Another time he saw a man walk by outside his room and asked me, "Is that Kevin?" It wasn't. Kevin was another of Frank's co-workers from years before, and he had been fired. Though the firing wasn't Frank's fault, he somehow felt that he could have done more to help his friend. These broken relationships were on his mind even then.

But Frank became the most emotional when he thought about his children. When I asked him what I could do to help Wendi, who lived in Tennessee, he simply said, "My poor baby."

I realized that I needed help preparing the boys for what was ahead. I asked one of the Calvary chaplains, an Orthodox priest, Fr. John, if he could meet with my family. He graciously agreed. The staff helped Frank into a wheelchair, and we gathered in the meeting room. Micah was ten, and Martin almost nine. Frank told them, "As long as you listen to your mother, you will always be protected." The children didn't say much. We all cried. Fr. John commended us for getting together to discuss the inevitable. He said that we were one of the very few families who have asked for his help in this way. He gave us confidence that we were doing everything we could.

Frank's pain was well controlled, and I sometimes wondered if the morphine had affected his mental state, or if he really was seeing things that I couldn't see. Several times he mentioned that two black priests had come to visit him. He called them "The Twins" because they looked alike. On more than one occasion he told me they were in the room with us, but I couldn't see them. Once he told me, "I'm looking down over your head."

Raquel Isaza came many times and sat by his bed while he slept, praying the Chaplet of Divine Mercy or sketching pictures of his peaceful, thinning face. When he awoke, she had already left, yet he would ask me, "Where's Roxy?"

Our friend, David Burns, came. The last time we had seen him was at Mariano Rivera's restaurant, Mo's New York Grill in New Rochelle, New York, not far from where David lived. Frank loved the great Yankee pitcher, so he wanted to celebrate our fifth wedding anniversary there. We invited David to join us. He came and gave us two wooden cross necklaces as gifts, but didn't stay long. Four years later when Frank became ill, David and I exchanged emails. When David learned that he may never see his friend again, he came to Calvary and sat at the foot of Frank's bed praying the rosary. They never spoke. Frank slept the whole time David was there.

My sister Susan, Frank's "Secret Fraternity Sister," wrote about her visits:

The hospital [was] ten blocks from my house. I could walk there to see him. Proximity is a big deal in New York City. Frank rallied (as my father and sister before him had rallied). I cancelled the winter semester classes I signed up for and went to see him as often as possible after work...One day as I walked into his room, he looked up and said, "Yo, Suzy Wooz, I've been thinking a lot about you."

"You have," I said.

"Yes," he said, "because you're following. Not many people would take the risks you're taking. You're going back to school. You found something you love." Listening to him speak to me as if it were the beginning, as if he weren't really dying, as if his participation in life, in my life, were going to continue, was just a marvel. It was comfortable. It was familiar. It was a gift. And I knew it.

Sometimes during these visits Frank cried a lot, "Take care of my kids," he said.

"Okay," I said.

Sometimes we laughed. "Yo, Suzy, do you have a razor blade?"

"I'm not giving you a razor blade."

"Com'on Suzy, you know you can trust me."

"It's not a problem of trust. You're on morphine. It's not safe."

"Then give me that straw."

"Okay." He cleaned his nails.

"Oh," I said, "I'm really glad I didn't give you the razor blade."

My brother Paul had come from Rochester and stayed with Susan and Jonathan. He made frequent trips to the hospital. Frank told Paul how much he had learned from him, watching him fight so hard to regain his strength after his near-fatal car accident.

My nephew, Peter, came. Frank had snapped the picture in defiance of the rules at Peter's first communion. Frank asked him, "I'd like you to mentor my sons on how to be respectful to their elders because that really means a lot to me."

Frank also went through a dark period where he was convinced that the medical staff was planning to euthanize him. When I left him at the end of the day, he would raise his hand, wave at me and say, "Good bye, my love." Sometimes he was so agitated that he would call me in the middle of the night, filled with panic and fear. This went on for a few days until, one afternoon, the physical therapist came into his room and asked why he had a scowl on his face.

I explained that Frank thought the staff had it in for him.

The therapist, an expressive Middle Eastern man, put all his energy into persuading Frank that the opposite was true. "Do you know how much it costs to keep you in this bed for one day?" he asked. "Thousands of dollars. If they wanted to kill you, they would've done it a long time ago to save money."

"That's a good point," Frank said.

The therapist also commented on all the visitors Frank received, "Never in my life have I seen a man as loved as you are." And then he recalled the day he witnessed Marshall's mother, Bobby Ann, sitting next to me at Frank's bedside. "The women that I know in that situation fight with each other. They don't get along. You are a blessed man."

Frank had always particularly loved to meditate by imagining the scenes of peace promised in the Biblical prophesies, like the baby playing with the serpent, and the lion lying down with the lamb. The love he shared had an ability to make peace and heal wounds that, in many other lives, tend to fester. For example, his oldest son, Marshall, who had been abandoned by his father through much of his youth, would later say, with great love and compassion, that, during his childhood, Frank "was growing up and learning how to be a man, and he had his share of learning experiences that caused him not to be around a lot of the time. But [...] wherever I did get to see my dad, he made every attempt possible to express his love for me and apologized for not being there when I needed him so much." Marshall referred to Micah and Martin, his beloved little brothers as "gifts." All around Frank, love was healing the wounds of his past.

"You Don't Argue with the Truth"

During these days, our CL community's annual three-day cultural festival, the New York Encounter, was in full swing. For obvious reasons, Frank and I couldn't be there, yet, in some way, we were there. Frank and I appeared on the big screen in a documentary marking the 60th anniversary of Communion and Liberation, *The Beautiful Road*. Frank was filmed giving a witness about his life, and I appeared singing with the choir. We were also present through prayer and offering, particularly for Jonathan as he presented his musical dance composition, *Adam Danced*. Mass was celebrated by Sean Cardinal O'Malley, Archbishop of Boston, and offered for Frank. Many of our friends from other parts of the country, and even the world, were in New York City for the big weekend. This afforded out-of-towners the opportunity to come and visit Frank in his final days. Among them were Ewa Chrusciel and Eric DeLuca, a couple from New Hampshire who were struggling to overcome certain obstacles in order to get married. One was that Eric was Jewish and Ewa a Catholic. They came to see us on Saturday, January 17th. Frank and I spoke with them for over an hour, a true tour de force for Frank, who poured out his energy without reserve for his friends. I was amazed at his sense of humor and ability to remember very specific details from our life together. He counseled them: "It's important that you do the best that you can because He [God] is governing all things, believe it or not... He loves you so much. He made this world for you. He already has the things He needs. He made this world for you, and He wanted to see how you would operate under these circumstances."

Frank began to cry, "I never guessed that this is what my vocation would be, laying up in some bed, watching the four walls."

But Frank did not want pity, and added: "Every tear that I shed is for you, nothing for me. Whatever happens from this day on, and even before that, was meant for you, not for me."

"Why not for you, too?" Eric asked.

Frank spoke with certainty: "Because my blessings come from exposing the love that God is showing us that He has for us."

He started speaking to God, "Ewa and Charles will always be with me. [...] I'm praying to You, Heavenly Father, that You touch this couple, that You show them what it takes to really sacrifice for Your love because it's important that they have it."

"You said, 'Ewa and Charles'," I told him.

"That's my grandfather's name," Eric chimed in; he felt like Frank was on to something. He was Eric, "Son of Robert, who is son of Charles." Eric explained how the Hebrew people didn't have last names. "They just say, 'Eric, Son of Robert, Robert, son of Charles.' They just keep it simple in the Bible."

"Yeah, I'm quite aware of that." Frank said, and laughingly told the story of how he had bought the Bible on DVD, thinking it would help him study God's Word,

244

only to fall into pages of genealogy. "I thought I knew everything. I didn't even know what 'begat' meant! I was like, next page… So I skipped ahead a few pages, and it was still going!" Then he looked at Eric, seriously: "Wow! It goes a very long way. You have quite a history!"

"Until somebody begat Frank," Eric said.

"Yeah, it's true," Frank said, "You don't argue with the truth."

Frank was growing tired. Ewa and Eric left, and, later that afternoon, my cousin, Derrick, came. He had flown in from Rochester, New York just to see his ailing friend. Frank had never forgotten how Derrick had opened his home to him and his groomsmen in the days before our wedding. When Derrick entered the room, Frank made a fist and raised his hand in the air: "D!"

The next day, Sunday, January 18th, was the last day of the New York Encounter. Friends from Boston and Washington, D.C. came to see Frank, but the visits were a sharp contrast to the day before. Frank could no longer speak, and his breathing was labored. We prayed and sang around his bedside. Friends stayed with him while I attended Mass in the community room.

When evening came, so did Marshall. We watched the NFC Championship—the Green Bay Packers versus the Seattle Seahawks—on Frank's TV. There wasn't much to say. Marshall and I both knew it wouldn't be long. I was surprised how frightened I became when Marshall left. I ran to the chaplain's office. Fr. John was there. "I think my husband is going to die very soon," I said, "Would you come and sit with us?"

"Sure," he said.

We prayed the rosary at Frank's bedside.

Around 11 p.m., the New York Encounter spilled into Frank's room. There were so many people that many were standing in the hallway. We prayed together, and, when we finished, Frank, who had been fighting for each breath, started struggling to speak.

Jonathan yelled, "Get the nurse! He can't breathe!"

The nurse came and said there were too many people in the room.

One by one, people started leaving, until there were just a few remaining. I asked Regina to stay with me, and everyone else left. The doctor came into the room and told us, "He is now actively dying. It could be three hours; it could be three days."

I couldn't imagine three days of counting each breath as it shook his entire body. Regina told me to try and get some sleep. I lay down in the reclining chair while she sat on the other side of his bed. I woke up around 5 a.m. Regina was asleep at Frank's head, and he continued his heavy breathing. I woke her up and told her I was going downstairs to get a cup of coffee. When I came back upstairs, I finished the coffee, but couldn't keep my eyes open. I lay in the recliner again, and fell in and out of sleep. My pain was excruciating. I needed some fast help.

When I was a postulant in the Missionaries of Charity, I had learned to pray "a flying novena"—Nine *Memorares*, an ancient prayer asking for the Virgin Mary's intercession for a particularly urgent need. I whispered the prayer, counting on my fingers, and asked Mother Teresa, "Please, Mother, don't let this go on much longer. Either allow Frank to get up from that bed and come home with me, or lead him home to Jesus." After saying, "Oh Mother of the Word Incarnate, despise not my petition" for the ninth time, a beam of light came in the window and landed on Frank. I looked over at him. He started to speak, but I couldn't understand what he was saying. I tried to get up, but couldn't. I felt like something was holding me down. Frank seemed to be breathing normally, and his face was peaceful. I lost the sense of urgency to rush to his beside. I waited a few more minutes, then got up and touched my hand to his lips. They were cold!

"Regina, wake up!" I said. "Frank snuck out on us."

Regina stirred from her sleep, "What?"

"He stopped breathing," I said. "Isn't that just like him, to sneak out on us like that?"

She took his pulse and confirmed it, then went to get the doctor, who pronounced him dead at 7:25 a.m. on Monday, January 19, 2015, a federal holiday, Martin Luther King, Jr. Day.

There was so much peace in that room, that I couldn't shed a tear. I kept saying, "You made it, Baby! You made it!" in complete amazement at how Frank was true to himself, right up to the very end. He didn't want a big drama surrounding his departure. He left unnoticed, on a beam of light.

When I told Tiffiny, who would live another year and a half, that I had no urge to cry, she said, "That's because there were so many angels in that room, there was no space for sorrow." (Tiffiny died in Cleveland, OH on August 5, 2016, after many stints in hospitals and rehabs.)

Phone calls were made, and people came. I had provided Calvary with the name and number of the funeral home, and they sent for the mortician, who came immediately and asked us to leave the room. When we came back in, Frank's body was zipped in a black body bag and lay on a stretcher. His feet looked so tall compared to his very thin body, which seemed only a few inches high.

"At the Hour of His Death"

They put my baby
in a body bag
and wheeled him away,
but he'd already gone.
He slipped out
on a ray of light
that reached
through the window.
I didn't even know
he'd gone
till I touched
cold lips
to the palm
of my hand.
(How fast the mouth gets cold
though the body stays warm.)
The angels gathered round
to comfort us.
No one screamed.
It seemed Lazarus
had been raised
before we had a chance
to cry.

"A Servant Leader"

The peace continued. I gave the mortician Frank's suit — one of the many he had bought before we were married, the same one he wore the last time he held the cross on Good Friday. "It's not going to fit him," I said, apologetically, "He's lost so much weight, and there's a button missing."

"That's not a problem; I'll pin it and he'll look fine," the man said.

He allowed me to ride in the service elevator as he transported Frank's body.

Because it was Martin Luther King Day, the boys were home from school with my mother. That's when it hit me. I had to face the most difficult moment of all—how to tell them their father had died. "Mommy has to tell you something." Their faces were so innocent. How could I break their hearts? Frank was the one who was good in moments like this. Now it was up to me. "Daddy went home to Jesus this morning."

They cried.

"But he's always going to be with us, just not in the same way." My words were like a house of straw in front of the big, bad news. They retreated to their bedroom. Thankfully, all my family members were around to support us. My niece, Erin, came over and entertained them. My brother David took them out for pizza. We discovered that Micah had strep throat, so Regina took him to the doctor. I was so agitated that, when she asked me for the doctor's address, I told her to look it up on Google. I knew I was being unreasonable, but I was on circuit overload. Still, I was grateful to have such a large family and so many friends who stepped forward and gave the boys much needed attention.

Giorgio Vittadini, my friend from Italy, came to see me that morning, accompanied by Olivetta Danese, from the *Memores* house, and Letizia Bardazzi, an Italian friend who was in New York for the Encounter. She told me, "You have to come to Italy."

It sounded like a great idea. When Frank got sick, we had planned to make a trip to Fr. Giussani's grave in Milan. We even got passports for the boys, but never made it.

"It feels strange not to have to say, 'Let me check with my husband,'" I told her.

I shared how Frank had me taking dictation just three days before he died, and read some excerpts from my marble notebook, "The rules we have are beneficial. If you can, get them from Fr. Rich." Giorgio laughed.

"Now Frank can read your mind," he said with a smile. From that moment on, my thoughts were a constant, effortless prayer.

When the funeral director, Frank Prospero, came to the house to discuss the details of Frank's send-off, I learned that a husband and wife burial plot would cost around $6,000.00, more than half the money I would receive from his life insurance. I wouldn't have enough money to cover the remaining costs. There was another option. Years ago, Frank's parents had purchased a companion plot in Pinelawn Memorial Park in Farmingdale, and since his father had remarried after Christalia's death, his second wife had made other burial arrangements. Frank was the obvious candidate for the unused space where the headstone had "SIMMONDS" engraved on it.

Months ago, I had asked him if he wanted to be buried with his mother, or with me.

"What do I care? I'll be dead!"

"Well, you should have some sort of a preference," I said.

He thought about it. "With you," he said.

Since I was the one who had pushed the issue, I wasn't that haunted by going against his wishes. I made plans to have Frank buried with his mother.

The viewing was the day before the funeral. Rather than sit around Frank's body and make small talk, I wanted to sing and hear what Frank meant to the people who came. Chris Vath gathered a group of musicians and handed out song sheets. Between musical numbers, various friends and family members got up and shared memories. Bobby Tannenhauser spoke about Frank's reliability and positive spirit at work. Pastor Ben McKnight witnessed to how Frank had become "a servant leader" who "always gave God the credit" and "would not let sickness stop him from what he wanted to do." Frank's friend, Rondu, called Frank "calm and cordial" in the way he helped, not only with computers, but also life lessons. He added: "Frank was a guy, when we talked, he kept it real." Our friend, Patricia Byrne, who had invited my whole family to her home out in Montauk, Long Island when Frank was sick, read a poem that her daughter, Eleanor, had written called "Change of Light." My godson, Anthony, who was just eight years old, stood before the whole room, pointed to the ceiling and said, "Frank, I hope you hear me in Heaven because I love you very much." He started to cry as he told us, "He was like a father to me, like the father that I had."

Chris Vath, who was the master of ceremonies, asked me to get up and speak. I told everyone how Frank's big-heartedness had expanded my own capacity to love. He loved so many people, and he loved them intensely. By accepting the love he had for others, I also got the chance to love the people that he loved. His love was so powerful and personal, it almost seemed exaggerated. He would tell someone, "I offer all my suffering for you," and then he would turn around and tell someone else the same thing. How was it possible? Frank taught me something about the love of Christ, the love of God-made-man.

The next day, January 22, 2015, was the funeral. It was held at our parish, St. Mary Mother of Jesus. Ten priests concelebrated, and the church was packed. Fr. Rich was the main celebrant, and Fr. Peter Cameron gave the homily. Pastor Ben McKnight's wife, Beverly, sang, as did the CL choir, and my brother-in-law Ken gave the tribute at the end.

Fr. Peter opened his homily with these words:

When we met this man, Frank Antonio Simmonds, we met a miracle.

Whether you knew him from the harrowing days of his youth, or via the Internet's many "Frank Speak" videos posted on YouTube, or in the gift of friendship unfailingly blessed with such joyful, childlike tenderness, those shining eyes, that handsome face, and an infectious sense of humor, who could help but be struck by the exceptionality of Frank Simmonds?

Father Luigi Giussani, Servant of God, the Founder of the ecclesial Movement Communion and Liberation—which Frank devotedly followed and led in New York—once wrote:

A miracle is an event that irresistibly calls the human being back to his Destiny, back to Christ, back to the living God (Why the Church?, p. 219).

That's what happened to us when we met Frank.

Because it was not possible to look at Frank— especially if you knew his history—without wondering: What could make him be that way?

But the "what" of our wondering is really a "Who."

It was encountering in Frank a different humanity. Commenting on this, the President of Communion and Liberation, Fr. Julián Carrón, says:

When a person bumps into a different humanity, it is something absolutely simple; it does not need to be explained but only to be seen, intercepted. It arouses wonder, awakens emotion, calls us back, moves us to follow by the strength of its correspondence with the structural longing of the heart.

That is to say, it calls us back to the Man whose own unique exceptionality is the source of the very possibility of a different humanity in the world: it calls us back to Jesus Christ.

During the funeral mass, I was smiling. My husband was being honored like a king. I drove my own car to Long Island for the burial and led the singing at the gravesite. Many people assumed that the shock hadn't hit me yet and I would soon crack up.

The following day, I sat in the crying room at St. Mary's and prayed my Seven Sorrows rosary as I had done every day in the final months of Frank's illness, since the night that Frank had prayed seven Hail Mary's over my heart. When I got to the end, I began asking Our Lady, "Why don't I feel a terrible loss?" I prayed the final prayer, "Oh Mary, who was conceived without sin, and who suffered for us..." I stopped. It was clear. She suffered for me, so I wouldn't have to.

Losing Frank's physical presence did bring an immediate change, which helped me to better understand why Frank had run to the hospital with his camera when his brother, Tony, died. There are no more memories to record once the person has passed on. I tried to express this change in a villanelle, "You Can't Take the Dead":

Photos are memories awakened
with borders for colors that bleed
The living can only be taken

positioned or snapped in creation
expanding wide angles undreamed
Photos are memories awakened

recording a life in its making
framing the best that's been seized.
The living can only be taken

through lenses in focus, not shaken
by movement that time guarantees.
Photos are memories awakened.

An image that fades unmistaken
moves out of the frame that we freeze.
The living can only be taken

No camera can capture what's vacant.
No flash can expose what's deceased.
Photos are memories awakened.
The living can only be taken.[24]

Still I asked my friend, David Galalis, to take pictures at Frank's wake and funeral. He took many beautiful photos of friends and family praying at Frank's coffin. I saw an outpouring of love, and a new type of communication unfolding.

As the days went by, I did have moments when I came undone, particularly when it came to the boys. Raising our children, I used to often step back and let Frank handle the discipline. Now it was up to me. Their acts of disobedience sent me through the roof. Yet I had to understand that they, too, were adjusting. Frank's death was a "Game Changer":

Every day, the chase commenced.
Their father ran them round the room.
A couple laps to build suspense—
he could have caught them in one loop.
He'd grab and roll them like a log
and launch the tickling poke attack.
Their laughter loud, it shook the house.
It shakes us now. It rolls us back—

A plot upturned gets filled in fast
but leaves a ghostly gap.

Our oldest son who needs to please
has lost all will to play.
His little brother loves the game
but runs without a chase.

---

[24] Rita A. Simmonds, "You Can't Take the Dead," *Presence: A Journal of Catholic Poetry*, 2019, p. 114.

Our dining room has been undone
and yet it looks the same.[25]

Still, I experienced Frank's help in unconventional ways. When the car needed repair, I asked Frank to help me and saw a light coming from his dresser. I opened the drawer to find a flashlight shining on a pile of papers. I went through them and found the address of a mechanic Frank used. On another occasion, the car got stuck in ice and snow. I couldn't even shovel it out. "Frank, you gotta help me," I said. No sooner had I cried out, than a man came and drove his car out of the space in front of me. I was able to drive the car straight into his space and then pull out. But the biggest help was just knowing he was with me all the time. I never felt that he was gone.

---

[25] Rita A. Simmonds, "Game Changer," *The Remembered Arts Journal*, Fall 2017.

Afterword

When Frank and I got engaged, in the Spring of 2003, our friend, Simonetta Wiener organized a little party for us after the weekly School of Community meeting that I'd been attending at Sacred Hearts and Saint Stephen's Church in Carroll Gardens, Brooklyn. When it came time for the toast, our friend Bill Fredrickson raised his glass of champagne and said, "Here's to fecundity!"

"Fecundity! What's that?" Frank said. He was not about to toast to something he didn't know the meaning of.

Various definitions were thrown out—fertility, fruitfulness, growth, offspring.

Frank got the idea, and I think it frightened him at the time.

Two days before Frank died, in his last long conversation with friends, he said, "Marriages don't come unless there's some sort of a sign showing you...what's the word, Honey?"

"Fecundity," I said.

"Fecundity," he repeated.

After our eleven and a half years of marriage, Frank understood the definition of that word because he lived it, and Frank's life continues to produce the hundredfold.

Tributes to
Frank Simmonds

Funeral Homily for Frank Antonio Simmonds

Fr. Peter John Cameron, O.P.

Saint Mary Mother of Jesus Church, Brooklyn, NY
January 22, 2015

Scripture Readings:
Lamentations 3:17-26
Colossians 1:24-29
John 14:1-6

When we met this man, Frank Antonio Simmonds, we met a miracle.

Whether you knew him from the harrowing days of his youth, or via the Internet's many "Frank Speak" videos posted on YouTube, or in the gift of friendship unfailingly blessed with such joyful, childlike tenderness, those shining eyes, that handsome face, and an infectious sense of humor, who could help but be struck by the exceptionality of Frank Simmonds?

Father Luigi Giussani, Servant of God, the Founder of the ecclesial Movement Communion and Liberation—which Frank devotedly followed and led in New York—once wrote:

A miracle is an event that irresistibly calls the human being back to his Destiny, back to Christ, back to the living God (*Why the Church?*, p. 219).

That's what happened to us when we met Frank.

Because it was not possible to look at Frank—*especially* if you knew his history—without wondering: *What could make him be that way?*

But the "what" of our wondering is really a "Who."

It was encountering in Frank a *different humanity.* Commenting on this, the President of Communion and Liberation, Fr. Julián Carrón, says:

> *When a person bumps into a different humanity, it is something absolutely simple; it does not need to be explained but only to be seen, intercepted. It arouses wonder, awakens emotion, calls us back, moves us to follow by the strength of its correspondence with the structural longing of the heart.*
>
> *That is to say, it calls us back to the Man whose own unique exceptionality is the source of the very possibility of a different humanity in the world: it calls us back to Jesus Christ.*

I.

Yet it wasn't always this way for Frank.

In fact, if we reflect on the perilous circumstances and consequences of the young Frank's life choices, we realize that *this* day really "should" have occurred many years before today.

We heard in the first reading a lament that could have been the youthful Frank's:

> *My soul is deprived of peace, I have forgotten what happiness is; I tell myself my future is lost, all that I hoped for from the Lord. The thought of my homeless poverty is wormwood and gall.*

Frank confessed that, in his words, "there were times that were bad when I wasn't even sure that I was a human being anymore."

After the devastating loss of his beloved mother when he was but a teenager, and opting then for a self-destructive lifestyle that he described as "deciding to follow myself," Frank made the conscious decision to turn his back on God.

As he put it: "I lost faith in God at that moment. I chose not to be aware of God."

All the same—because *so great is God's faithfulness*—at a moment in 1981 when Frank's life and prospects looked particularly bleak, he was moved—*inspired*—to write this poem which he entitled "Lord, Show Me the Way:"

I pray for a good future. God, please overlook my past.
Forgive my sins so I can find happiness at last.
I am a lost sheep. Please lead me back to the herd.
Help me change my life, Lord; just bless me with Your Word.
I'm paying for my mistakes. Please, help me ease the pains.
Release me from the anxiety of my spirit being in chains.
I love you so much, God. Your Son dealt with pain and strife.
I'm thankful that Jesus, for our sins, had given up His life.
You're so understanding, so willing to forgive.
Please cleanse my mind and body, so my spirit can live.
Reality has set in; I know I've done wrong.
My heart is filled with sorrow;

it's for Your forgiveness that I long.
I feel I'm unworthy to ask You for this blessing.
You know it took me very long to have to learn my
lesson.
But I will not give up to Satan the life You've given
me.
Please send the Holy Spirit as my guide, until I come
to Thee.

It was that poem that saved Frank from the otherwise inevitable fate of a lengthy incarceration. He was mercifully sentenced to a rehab instead.

How was it that Frank was able to write such a poem? Maybe it is owing to the fact that, at another very dark and desperate moment in Frank's life, a priest—out of nowhere—approached Frank and said, "If you ask God, he will reach into the gutter and pull you out."

For some door began to reopen once Frank got to rehab. And, as Frank would later confess, "Conversion is meeting something exceptional."

And it was there in rehab that Frank's future wife Rita, who by this point had met Frank amidst his tribulations, sent Frank a letter along with an image of the Blessed Virgin Mary.

In the letter, Rita wrote, "I love you; I care about you."

And Frank recalled, "Sometimes you meet something that defies everything that you think you believe in. Rita just looked at the person and cared about the person."

As one of Frank's heroes, Pope Saint John XXIII, expressed it: "I have looked into your eyes with my eyes. I have put my heart near your heart."

And Frank said, "This is when things began to change."

This is the event that Frank lived from for the rest of his life.

No wonder, then, that toward the end of his life Frank's whole being was ardently, passionately fixed on the love of God and the breathtaking power of that love…a love that he proclaimed to be "greater than suffering."

Frank practically begged us:

Love without conditions and pray. Acknowledge that you do not want to be part of the evil of the world, that you want to do something positive—not just for yourself but for everyone.

II.

Frank modeled that love in the way he did his job.

Frank was a doorman in New York City—a menial job, you might say, not measuring up to Frank's real potential.

But Frank loved and lived his job as a vocation, patterned on the original Door-man, Jesus Christ, who says of himself in the Gospel of John:

I am the gate. Whoever enters through me will be saved, and will come in and go out and find pasture (Jn 10:9).

In today's Gospel—words that Jesus speaks just hours before he dies—we hear our Savior plea:

Do not let your hearts be troubled. In my Father's house there are many dwelling places. I go and prepare a place for you.

The choice of this Gospel would be very dear to Frank because Frank always talked about the Father's house and how there were plenty of rooms in it for everyone.

The very way in which Frank would open that door and let residents and guests into that building where he worked was the concrete, personal sign to them of another, heavenly house where they were awaited and would be welcomed…a welcome that began in the gaze Frank gave to everyone who crossed his path.

III.

But then came the diagnosis of terminal cancer.

For a person of lesser faith, hope, and love, the news would have been devastating…a reason to give up.

But that is not how Frank responded. Rather, he said:

Cancer put me in a position where my needs were in front of me. I learned to depend on Something Greater than myself. Because I don't change reality. Who can give me the joy that can't be taken away?

This is the glorious mystery proclaimed by today's second reading:

Now I rejoice in my sufferings for your sake, and in my flesh I am filling up what is lacking in the afflictions of Christ on behalf of his body, which is the Church.

Frank made the deliberate, fully intentional decision to make the best use of his suffering for the good of others. He professed:

As for me, my way is offering up all my pain, my suffering, all of myself for the world. I do this voluntarily, willingly. That is the greatest freedom that a person can ask for. I offer everything to you, God, because only you can take this and bless the world. Suffering has a meaning.

This is why Frank was so thrilled and took such delight in carrying the cross across the Brooklyn Bridge for CL's annual Way of the Cross on Good Friday. That is what is depicted on Frank's memorial card, and it is photographs like that one that appeared in the newspapers right after the event.

Frank contacted one of his friends from the past—a cynical individual who was against religion and was opposed to Frank's conversion.

Frank asked him, "Did you see the picture in the paper of me on the Brooklyn Bridge with the cross?"

His negative friend replied, "What I saw was some black dude carrying some wood with a whole bunch of white people behind him."

Yet here we still are—behind Frank…following the way he traced out for us.

At the point of the deepest desperation in his life, Frank made this promise to God: "If You keep me from what I am about to do, I will serve You for the rest of my life!"

We are here today because Frank kept his promise. And we are in awe because Frank's witness shows us that serving God is the source of the greatest possible happiness in life.

Pope Francis has written:

To those who suffer, God does not provide arguments which explain everything; rather, his response is that of an accompanying presence (*Lumen Fidei* #57).

All Frank ever asked of us in his suffering was to accompany him…to be companions to others who suffer.

Let us honor the life of this holy man by being good companions to each other. Let us thank God for the priceless companionship of Frank Simmonds. And let us beg, as Pope Francis would move us, that our infinite sadness be cured by an infinite love (see *Evangelii Gaudium* #265).

That cure will come quick in the Infinite Companion who is about to become Present on this altar.

Eulogy at Frank's Funeral Mass

Kenneth Genuard

Saint Mary Mother of Jesus Church, Brooklyn, NY
January 22, 2015

Frank was a man so filled with the love of God that to know him was to become familiar with God. This is because he loved unconditionally and genuinely and he loved many, many people. At a certain point he was so filled with this love, he couldn't keep it just to his friends. In the end, when he entered his suffering, he felt compelled to love the entire world, like God.

He was not a perfect man, however. He was a human being full of mistakes, faults, and weaknesses and a past filled with a lot of bad decisions. But this is not what defined Frank but instead gives witness to the reality and power of Christ.

His was a tough road of hardships and suffering – some given to him and some brought on by himself. Yet the voice of God was always with him even in his darkest hour. Frank had never given up on that voice which spoke within the depths of his heart.

He lost his parents at a young age and his way to cope with this was to enter a life of drugs and crime on the streets. This is no secret. Frank never kept this a secret because later he realized that these things showed all the more how the power of God can save anyone. But even in his darkest hours, during his worst, (I didn't know Frank back then but I'm convinced that) Frank was never a bad man. Earl said yesterday "Frank was a good man." And that's how I remember him.

He was a man with an extremely strong will, but left an openness, a crack that allowed God to enter.

I'm sure you all heard his story of when living on the streets, at the end of himself, he recognized that the voice of God never completely left him, but came to him in a small whisper while he was contemplating jumping onto the train tracks. Then, as he described so movingly, that voice came out of his mouth – "Lord if you save me from this, if you let me live, I will serve you for the rest of my life." Looking back, it surely was the voice of the Other, for even he was surprised to hear himself say it. Then from that point on, he'd been running towards God. Running.

It wasn't too long after that he entered rehab to recover from his addictions. Soon he met his future wife Rita. Soon after getting married, Frank and Rita gave birth to two beautiful boys – Micah and Martin.

Once Frank became aware that God loved him and saved him and cared for him in such a personal, special way, he wanted to make everything right. He did his best to recover and mend the relationships with those he had neglected in the past.

I met Frank about a year before he got married to Rita. At the time, I was dating my wife Naomi. From the start, he and I hit it off. It was one of those friendships that make one feel as if we knew each other our whole lives. His complete embrace of me, his affection, and his simple friendship were so easy to accept. And from that point on, we were brothers. I didn't think our friendship would get any better than that, but it did.

Frank took a journey. He had travelled such a long way to get to this point. He had been through so much, had overcome so much, one would think he had simply arrived, but it really was the beginning of the journey.

While Frank always believed that God had a special love for him and all people, he considered it mostly a private affair. When he met Rita's friends and family and encountered this community of CL, he at first put his arm up in defense. I remember him saying to me "Ken, that's cool that you guys do School of Community and want to read Father Giussani; just as long as you don't bring it over in my direction, then everything's going to be cool."

But while he maintained this attitude he always allowed himself to stay in relationship with people who challenged him – first of course, his wife, but others as well. Then he began to realize that his faith and the love that God had for him can grow into fatherhood by being shared, by being given to others, by belonging to a people. This was a step that Frank slowly but surely took. And once he took it, his personal change was meteoric. At a certain point, I was leading our small group of school of community in Bay Ridge and circumstances were such that it was best that I did not continue. So I "tossed the keys" to Frank and he then took us to the stars. The way he embraced this experience was miraculous. I've never seen anyone change so fast. Very soon, Frank and the love of God became a public affair which he shared with everyone. He led our SoC, helping us all to be more real, more honest and we watched his faith in Christ grow before our eyes. All of us were attracted by his certainty in Christ's love and his powerful way of communicating this!

Soon after, we needed a new responsible for the New York community and when I was asked who should fill the role, I did not hesitate to mention Frank. Unfamiliar as he was with it, he took it. He then gave countless witnesses at vacations, community days, encounter events, personal meetings, and even travelled around the country to tell his conversion story. He was a man with a mission and he touched many hearts - even around the globe as people in other countries began to hear his story and be moved by his witness.

Once Frank said Yes to Christ it brought him to do things he never wanted or thought he would do. For example, he never liked to read long books and then found himself reading the books of Father Giussani faithfully for School of Community. He never liked following people, and then found himself following those who he saw brought him closer to God. He used to say to me "Diggity, I follow you. You are a sign of God's love for me and I thank God for you every day." He even sang a song for me at my 40th birthday party in front of a room full of guests – something he told me that he was always terrified of doing. He was a changed man.

But, for me, the witness that gave the most glory to God was the one he gave in front of the passion of his illness. From the start Frank accepted this and continued to trust that God had his best interests in mind. While suffering greatly, he spoke with more certainty of God's love and care for him and kept affirming his belonging to Christ through the people that were given to him. At a certain point, he saw every single person in his life as a sign of God, as a sign of the love of Christ. For him, his faith deepened to the point where there was no separation between the flesh and the divine. And this filled him with gladness, gratitude and love.

We know how much Frank suffered, not only physically, but also through the mental anguish of navigating through the medical system to get the care he needed. His hope was at times brought up and then dashed down in a moment. We know how he had been run ragged going here and there to get his testing and treatments. Throughout all of this he admitted how hard it all was, but in the same breath affirmed that he is in God's hands and that we are all loved with an unimaginable love. He was positive not because he was a positive thinker but because he had an awareness that the Mystery was "behind all of this" and cared infinitely for His creation. He trusted in this which made him a presence to everyone he met. This gave him such an intelligence that people young and old went to him for counsel or just to be in his warm, comforting presence. He became a spectacle to many. All those who he came in contact with loved him. Even at his job where he worked as a doorman, the people who lived in the building looked forward to seeing his face every day. Frank gave hope, comfort, and friendship to countless people.

At the end of his life he continually offered up his sufferings to God for his friends and for all humankind. There he became one with Christ and shared in His passion. This was his greatest witness. He was aware of the love God had for him to the end and how important it was to communicate that to all those around him.

Pray for us, Frank, that we may have your faith in God's eternal love for us and become witnesses like you!

Frank, Future Leader

Giorgio Vittadini

This article appeared in Il Sussidiario,
January 23, 2015.

It is said that the things that change the fate of the world are the most glaring or obvious. However, many times the beginning of something new is subtle, but as real and unavoidable as the growing grass. Monday morning, at the end of a long illness, in Brooklyn, not far from where a few weeks earlier a policeman was killed in a clash during inflamed racial tensions in America, Frank Simmonds, one of many African-Americans in New York and one of the many who suffer, died.

His human story is really not just another among many, but indeed there is something special, particularly in a time in the history of the US and the world in which it seems increasingly difficult for different races and religions to coexist. Frank was happily married; he had four children whom he adored, and a regular job. But his past life was far from linear. He came from a middle-class family and at the age of seventeen his mother died of cancer. The illness and death of his mother seemed to Frank the culmination of a life that for him, as for many, lacked meaning. Drug use, the way he forgot the harshness of reality, quickly left him sharing life with the homeless, for almost ten years.

As for so many, his young life would have been wasted had Frank not met, almost by chance, a white woman named Rita. First a friendship was born among them, and then quickly it became a love anchored by the deeply rooted faith of this Christian woman. Frank found in Rita the desire to live again. She convinced him that recovery meant to take his health seriously. The journey was tough but Frank discovered, with faith in Christ, a comfort and a reason to fight. Overcoming his drug addiction, he found a job and married Rita.

His deep authenticity and his wonder so struck Rita's friends in the community of Communion and Liberation in New York, that they wanted Frank to be their responsible. They wanted to look at someone who knew he had received everything; one who lived with gratitude. "In his presence it was easier to feel free, to look at myself without measuring and calculating, as if there was some practical way to attain gusto, life (says Susan, a friend); No was able to recognize my freedom as he was."

From this marriage came two wonderful children, but the story was not like a Frank Capra film. The happy ending was not because things "went well." After a few years, Frank got cancer. And, it was in this situation that the entire fabric of his experience emerged: living the disease, working and living normally, his face the same as before, smiling, deep and peaceful, full of positivity, offering his suffering with simplicity as participation in the sacrifice of Christ.

Until the last couple days in the hospital where he was admitted, he did not stop thanking the doctors and nurses for their work, communicating peace and hope to relatives and friends as they remained in the devastating experience of the disease. He died the morning after the end of New York Encounter, a public cultural event organized by his friends in Manhattan, almost not wanting to disturb it, having offered his suffering for them. A posthumous Christmas story? No, that upsets the skepticism of a tired bourgeois society, even one that seems to unite against violence.

In the modern world where cynicism and nihilism seem to have already won, as the newspapers, television, and columnists seem to say, Frank represents an authentically new world, where the desire for happiness and the strength of faith are victorious; where there is no circumstance that determines the social life of man, there is no race that divides, no degradation that cannot be escaped, and no disease that can destroy hope.

Homily at the First Anniversary Mass for Frank Antonio Simmonds

Fr. Richard Veras

Saint Peter's Church, New York, NY
January 18, 2016

I want to offer some impressions, just some images, because just as the mystery of God can't be contained by the Gospels, He's infinite, but the Gospel stories give us windows into the Infinite. We are infinite desire, infinite need. We are made in the image of God, so a person's life cannot be captured, because a person's life is infinite. That's so much more evident when the person's life is united with Christ—when the begging part of Christ and the begging part of man, unite, become one.

A story that Frank told many times that many of you know, because Frank was very generous with his witness—it was 2 a.m. on a dark street, and Frank was desperate and he decided he was going to mug the next person that came down the street. The next person who came down that street at 2 a.m. was a priest. Every time I heard that story, I thought, What is that priest doing out at 2 a.m.? I'm pretty sure there was a hospital nearby; it was a hospital visit...Frank decides to show him mercy. It's all going to be okay as long as the priest keeps his mouth shut. But the priest doesn't do that. He says to Frank, "Young man, if you think God is going to come and lay down with you in the gutter, He won't. Do you know why? Because He's holy. But if you ask Him, He'll come and take you out of this gutter."

Every time I heard that story, and I've heard it so many times, I thought, who was that priest? Because it *never* would have been me. Who was that holy, saintly, courageous, confident priest? Because if I saw Frank in the distance, I would've turned around! And if I didn't see him until the last moment, I certainly wouldn't turn to challenge him. So who was that priest?

Years later, we're on a CL vacation in upstate New York, and there's free time—the pool, a soccer game, different things happening, and we were told there was a path to a waterfall. Frank asked me, "Fr. Rich, do you want to go to that waterfall?"

I said, "Yes, let's go."

We took a simple walk, and we spent some time at the waterfall. We might've been gone a half hour, and we didn't speak of anything hugely profound. We were just two friends walking to a waterfall. I thought, this is an impossible friendship. I thought about the holy priest. I'm taking the walk that that priest deserves to take. Jesus says, "You reap what you haven't sown." It was a beautiful, peaceful walk at a beautiful waterfall. Two friends who love each other. I thought, there's another priest out there somewhere who is supposed to take this walk. But God is merciful...the Year of Mercy—What a walk of mercy— God's mercy on Frank, who in his wildest dreams never thought he'd be at a hotel with his wife and children at a beautiful vacation, and that he'd have to take vacation time from his job to be with his wife and children, and I would be the last person to be the instrument of salvation for someone in Frank's position, or so I imagine. Maybe that priest never expected to be such either.

Many months later, Frank said, "What a beautiful walk that was!" It was so moving to me. Christ was present; we saw the same thing. It was objective. There was nothing

277

exceptional about that walk except that walk was the fruit of Christ's action in the world, in the flesh.

Another impression, Frank all through his witnesses would say, "When you recognize God in conversion, you realize He was there the whole time." It's not that He abandoned you, then showed up at your conversion moment. God was there the whole time. "Christ begging for the heart of man; man begging for the heart of Christ." So Christ was there at Frank's worst moments, begging for his heart. In fact, perhaps even through Frank's near despair, Frank's anger, Frank's calling out—that was Christ saying, "Please, keep begging for me! Keep begging!"

The Blackfriars Repertory Theatre was the occasion for Frank and Rita to meet. Our friend, Fr. Peter, wrote a play called "The Living Silence." The man who played Jesus was David, who introduced Rita and Frank. Rita's sister, Naomi, played Mary, who shows up at the end when the dead body of Jesus is placed in her arms. She's crying and she says, "How can this be?" which makes total sense. I can understand a mother saying that at the death of her son. "How can this be…" there's a pause, "since I do not know man?" In other words, even the dead body of my son is a miracle because I'm a virgin, and so this, the seemingly most evil act ever committed, is powerless in front of the fact of Christ. And then Mary goes on to say all the things that Mary said in the Scriptures, "Behold, the handmaid of the Lord; Let it be done to me according to Your Word." Then she recites the Magnificat with the dead body of Jesus in her arms. "My soul proclaims (present tense) the greatness of the Lord; my spirit rejoices in God my Savior. He has looked with favor on His lowly servant. From this day, all generations will call me blessed."

Frank reminds me of that amazing scene because of Frank's certainty. When you reach conversion, Christ is always there. Why could Frank give his witness so generously? It was so moving; it changed people's lives over and over again. Why could he revisit these very painful moments, for us, over and over again? Because they weren't dark moments of despair any longer. Frank had discovered Christ was there. "He was there, waiting for me…I may have been blind, but He was there waiting."

When Frank said, "When you recognize God in conversion, you realize He was there the whole time," he said that post conversion, after meeting Rita, after meeting Fr. Peter, after meeting Naomi. "Come to me."—his friends coming back with his family, which brings me to another impression: The poem that Frank wrote when he was in prison.

In part of that poem, he says, "Forgive my sins so I can find happiness at last./I am a lost sheep. Please lead me back to the herd." Mary was certain, because even though dead, this body of her Son came from her virgin womb. Where does Frank get the certainty to say, "When you recognize God in conversion, you realize He was there the whole time."? Because Frank was saved by Christ who is the Word made Flesh. Christ remains with us in a companionship. So as that body was so real for Mary, an undeniable fact, Frank's companionship that he met was for him an undeniable fact. So Frank, alone in prison, writes, "Forgive my sins so I can find happiness at last./I am a lost sheep. Please lead me back to the herd." Do you understand that you and I are the herd? Do you understand that you and I are the mercy that Christ had on Frank? Frank prayed that prayer, and Christ had us in his sight— our faces, our names, our particular love for Frank. Christ embraced Frank, not spiritually. He embraced him physically—Rita, David, Naomi, Peter, Marshall, Micah, Martin, Jonathan, Maryann, Ken…names after names after names. And so we witnessed the answer to an impossible prayer, created at an impossible moment in a man's life. So Frank's life witnesses that mercy is real; Christ's presence is real. It's for everyone. It's not reserved for a particular moment, it's not reserved for a person who's particularly spiritual; His mercy is real. He's really present.

And the last thing I want to speak about is the presence of Christ and what it means for us today celebrating this Mass. What it means, the way we conceive of Frank's place in our lives, Frank's presence in our lives.

The year that Frank spoke at New York Encounter, (the last three days of his life he offered his sufferings for New York Encounter), our friend, Christina, was giving a tour of an exhibit on Cardinal Newman. I went to that exhibit. It was very, very good. In the end, Christina finishes explaining all the panels, giving all the information, and she says to us, a mixed crowd, "There's one more thing I want to say. Cardinal Newman is my friend. Doing this exhibit, we've become friends." And I know that Christina is not a crazy person. That's so striking to me. Think of the Church. We speak of our saints in a totally different way than people speak of historical figures. We speak of Cardinal Newman, we speak of Fr. Giussani, we speak of St. Francis in a totally different way than we speak historically of George Washington or a scientist would speak of Albert Einstein. "He was great, a great inspiration, did a lot for the field." We speak of our saints and those we love in the present tense. "Cardinal Newman is my friend."

How is this possible? Why is it not just some sentimental theory? Jesus said to us, "I am with you always, until the end of the world." Frank discovered that when he said, "When you recognize God in conversion, you realize He was there the whole time." "I am with you always." The same Jesus when Paul was persecuting the Church, says, "Paul, why are you persecuting Me?"

"Who are you?"

"I am Jesus."

"So you are my disciples and we are one."

Where did Jesus say to His Father, "Pray for us."? Where did He intercede for us? The Church says He always intercedes for us to the Father. What was Jesus' prayer? "Father, where my disciples are, I also desire to be, that where they are, I may also be." And so we are in communion with Christ; we are united to Christ. He's present to us. It also means that Christ is united to us. "Where I am, my friends, my disciples, may also be." So if Christ says, "I am with you always, even to the end of the world," well, Christ married Himself to the Church. He is with his saints always; they are with Him always. If Christ is with us always, Frank is with us.

Fr. Giussani used to say that when a person dies, he is more present to you. It's hard to understand but I'm convinced it's true. I understand it to the core of my being. I'm convinced it's true because I believe Jesus; I believe those words, like Peter, when Jesus spoke about the Eucharist, "Where else will we go." I trust you.

St. Therese wrote letters to a seminarian, Maurice, and she said, "I'm going to die, but when I die, I'll be more present to you."

Maurice wrote back, "I believe you, but I can't really get my head around that."

So we are here, whether with a lot of faith or a little faith, rejoicing with Frank. Why are we rejoicing with Frank in this Year of Mercy? We are rejoicing with Frank because Christ tells us, salvation history tells us, the Psalms tell us, "Give thanks to the Lord for He is good; His mercy endures forever." If His mercy endures forever, it means those upon whom He has mercy, must live forever. Frank endures forever. We endure forever—eternal rejoicing in the endless mercy of God.

Fr. Giussani says, "God–the mystery, destiny made man–makes Himself present right now to you and to me, to all those who are called to see and recognize Him through a face: a new human face we run into."

Mercy has become flesh; mercy remains flesh through our faces, our lives, and with Frank we rejoice before this fact. "Give thanks to the Lord for He is good; His mercy endures forever." Jesus promises us. Jesus says, "Fear not, little flock," as he was saying to Frank, "Fear not, Frank. I'm sending someone. Fear not, Frank. Write that poem to me. Let's talk! I'm crying out for you; cry out for Me. Beautiful! Beautiful! Frank, you're praying to the herd. I have them all planned out. I have them because I have mercy on them. Frank, they're just as bad as you, I promise. And I have to have just as much mercy on them as I have on you, and once you meet each other, you're going to rejoice in that, now and forever because it gives Me even greater joy than it gives you."

So "His mercy endures forever." Our own communion endures forever. And so with Frank, with Cardinal Newman, with Fr. Giussani, with St. Therese, we rejoice at this vigil Mass, that even though I can't wrap my head around it, a year ago tomorrow, it was Christ's mercy that embraced Frank. And just as death had no power over Christ, so Mary remained certain. We can say that death has no power over our friend, and so we can say, "our souls proclaim the greatness of the Lord, our spirits rejoice in Christ our Savior, for he has looked with mercy on His lowly servants, and ages to come shall call us blessed for the almighty does great things for us, and holy is His Name."

Tribute at Frank's First Anniversary Mass

Marshall A. Simmonds

St. Peter's Church, New York, NY
January 18, 2016

First, I would like to thank everyone for being here today to pay tribute to a special man, a great friend, a wonderful father, and most importantly, an amazing person, Mr. Frank Simmonds. Your presence here at Saint Peter's means that you, too, were touched by his love and his genuine friendly spirit.

Exactly one year ago, we lost a really great guy. At least in my life, Frank was one of my favorite people in the world. I was his very first child, born thirty-seven years ago, in 1978 when the world was a different place—a lot less technology and a lot more time to bond with family. But as a young child, I wasn't able to spend as much time as I really wanted to with my dad. He was growing up and learning how to be a man, and he had his share of learning experiences that caused him not to be around a lot of the time. But one thing I've always known was that he loved me very much. Due to some unfortunate circumstances, I never had the opportunity to live full time with my father, but wherever I did get to see my dad, he made every attempt possible to express his love for me and apologized for not being there when I needed him so much.

My father was very sensitive when it came to the people he loved the most. When his mother unfortunately passed away while he was in high school, it pushed him into sort of a downward spiral that took him a while to recover from. Unfortunately, from my perspective, it meant he wasn't able to be around much during my childhood in the 1980s. But, like I said, when he did come to see me, it felt like we were together all along, the way he showed me love.

In most cases, not having your parents together while you're a child means you make excuses for yourself and expect pity from others, but Frank never wanted that from me. He always made sure that I accepted my own responsibility for my actions and blamed myself for my effort or lack thereof. He always told me that I can do anything that I put my mind to, and he would always be proud of me if I tried my best. I always took that into consideration when there was something tough to deal with in my life. And there were plenty of tough times to go around for me.

As I began to grow up into my teenage years, my dad was starting to put his life back together after dealing with a decade of addiction and law troubles. He would come to visit me a lot more at my grandmother's house on Long Island, and he would come pick me up to spend weekends with him at his apartment in Queens. He was always a really good father. He never let me disrespect him or my mother, and he was not afraid to remind me who was the father and who was the son.

As I got a little older as a teen, I thought I didn't have to follow the rules, and my Dad gave me a little dose of reality a couple times, and I really needed that from him. So even though, as a young child, he wasn't around to teach me certain things, when I needed him the most as a teen, he was right there handling his responsibility and molding me into a good man.

When I graduated from high school in 1996, my Dad was right there in the audience, and it felt so good to have him there for me.

As soon as I graduated, I went ahead and enlisted in the United States Army where I learned what being a man is all about. I realized that it takes a lot of mental strength to keep your emotions under control in order to serve a purpose and protect those who you care about the most. I realized that my father not being around while I was a child was sort of a blessing in disguise. He didn't want me to see him at his lowest points in life. He wanted to give me a strong example of a man to remember and to follow in his best footsteps.

At the age of twenty, I had my first child, my daughter, Daezhana who Frank really, really loved very much. And I can say he was a very good grandpa for her. She really loved her grandpa very much. He would come visit her all the time and made her feel so special and loved.

It was around that time that he married the love of his life, Rita, and soon after gave me one of the best gifts he could ever have given me, a little brother, Micah. A couple years later, he gave me a second gift, another little brother, Martin. And I must say, I really love those guys very much and I'll always be there for them as long as I live.

Thanks to my father, I was able to use his experiences to make a lot of good decisions in my life. He taught me how to love and how to treat everyone special on an individual basis.

Now I have my own son to take care of, and I have another son on the way in the next two months. It will be difficult to explain to them where their grandfather is, but I will make sure they know that he was a great man who loved them very much.

To his sisters, Emma and Althea, he also loved you very much, as well as his brother, Kenny, and his brother from another mother, Anthony. So even though we lost his physical presence, we all know that he will live forever in our hearts.

Rita, Micah and Martin, he loved you with all his heart, and now I will also love you forever, and I'll try my best to help you navigate through life without Frank.

I'd like to wish everyone a happy and healthy 2106, and thank you all for being here to remember my father, Frank Simmonds.

Tribute at Frank's Second Anniversary Mass

John Touhey

St. Peter's Church, New York, NY
January 16, 2017

My Friendship with Frank

I was—no, I am a friend of Frank Simmonds. In fact, that is what I would like to talk to you about—how Frank is a friend to me now.

First of all, thank you Rita for asking me to speak this morning. As I was thinking about what I wanted to say, one experience I did not have with Frank came to my mind; that is the experience of an awkward silence.

You know what I'm talking about, I'm sure. We have all experienced that awful moment when you're one on one with another person, usually someone you don't know very well (but it can also happen with someone you've known for 20 years, a dear friend, even a family member). You are having an ordinary conversation and suddenly everything comes to a halt. A silence falls and it just hangs there. Seconds may pass and the anxiety builds, until it becomes almost unbearable. This experience can be terrifying. And so you desperately try to fill up that nothingness that has revealed itself in the silence by grasping for a topic, any topic—the weather, sports, "How's so-and-so doing?" Or, in the worst cases, you make some pathetic excuse and slip away. I think we have all had this experience many times.

Frank and I did not see each other frequently. However, there were three occasions when I spent extensive periods of time with Frank alone, just the two of us. Twice when I was filming him for various media projects and then for a few remarkable hours in the hospital just before he died.

We joked around when we were working and, of course, the conversation in the hospital was much more profound. He was really looking directly at the face of God by that point and the things he said were prophetic and extraordinary. But on all three occasions what strikes me most of all now, in reflection, was what happened during the many lulls in conversation and the long moments of silence between us.

Those moments of silence with just about anyone else would have felt very uncomfortable. There would have been some anxiety and a temptation to fill up that silence. But with Frank, remarkably, it was not like that. The silences were not awkward and did not induce anxiety, because they were not empty, but full.

One of the times I was with Frank, we were supposed to be filming a scene for a film I was making. Only it started to rain, so we had to wait it out. Frank and I sat in my van and made some small talk and joked about our wives. But at a certain moment, we just sat there and listened to the rain falling on the roof and windshield. It was a very beautiful moment.

It is true that Frank said many extraordinary things to us, his friends. But, to me, even more striking was simply the way he was. Being with Frank was very peaceful in a sense because you knew you were with someone who was really there; he was totally present, with his whole self. It was clear in those silences that Frank truly experienced his existence as gift from God. And also that moment in time was a gift. And that he accepted my own presence with him as a gift. You can't fake being present. It isn't a trick you can learn from a book or a technique to be taught by an expert. That way of being that Frank had was the fruit of an awareness that was given to him by the Holy Spirit through his wife, his children, his friends, through the Church in the CL Movement and through the whole remarkable path of his life.

You know, Jesus is a genius. I think it was very significant that, toward the end of his life, He made Frank a doorman. We have to pay attention to that fact. I'm sure it was not a mistake. It was a sign from Jesus. What is the main task given to a doorman? It is to simply be there, to be present.

When I was with Frank at the hospital (this was during a period when he was in and out of consciousness), he told me that at some point in the previous days, he had experienced death. Frank told me that he had come face to face with the Lord, but Jesus told him that it was not time for him to die yet, because He still had things for Frank to do. There are so many people Jesus touched and helped through Frank when he was in his hospital bed—and also through the videos he made with Rita during the time of his illness. To me, he really was Jesus's doorman!

In my time with Frank, I had an experience of timelessness. You could even say it was a holy experience. In fact, when I was working at the New York Encounter this weekend, I spent a whole day off on my own completing a project for the final assembly. There were curtains separating the spaces and at one point, I heard two of the Encounter volunteers talking. One of the girls, a college student, was explaining to her friend about today's Mass and why we were gathering. She had never met Frank, but she was trying to tell his story. And she got it basically right—how Jesus had pulled Frank out of the gutter and transformed his life. For that girl, Frank's story was something vital to this moment that had to be shared.

Look, I'm sure Frank has zero interest in us "memorializing" him in the traditional sense. But memory isn't just recalling something lost in the past. Memory is also remembering a fact that affects you now. And this is one way Frank's friendship manifests itself in my life today. His witness provokes a question in me. It makes me ask myself, am I alive now? Am I present?

I have no idea what happens in Heaven. I can't imagine what it must be like; it is a complete mystery to me. But I do know one thing Frank is doing right now, because he told us when we were at the hospital. He said that he would be praying for us and when he prayed with us he asked for three things. First, that we would be aware of the presence of Jesus in our lives. Secondly, that we would be given the grace to live our friendship with Christ through the community He gave us. And thirdly, that we would be bold and go out into the world, announcing and sharing Jesus's friendship with everybody.

So, there is a clear way I can live my friendship with Frank right now—and that's to ask the Lord for the same things that Frank is asking on my behalf.

I'm a storyteller by vocation. They tell you that every story has a beginning, a middle, and an end. But my friendship with Frank did not end when I left that hospital room. Our friendship does not have an end. It has a destination, but not an end.

An Old Acquaintance

Theodore Oberman

February 11, 2015

New Year's Eve is an odd time. When one is young, trepidations abound over how late the night will go (the later the better); when old, there is the growing unease that another year has passed, ever so much faster. Even odder is the holiday's theme song, "Auld Lang Syne." It's an ode to the past, sung at a moment when one's thoughts are usually forward looking. That's the point of course, but it is strangely juxtaposed with the inevitable resolutions, dreams, and visions one has for the upcoming year, either spoken to others, or held silently for oneself.

This past New Year's Eve, a group of us spent the hours approaching midnight with Frank and Rita Simmonds at the hospice; Frank would pass from this world a few weeks later. The evening slipped by doing what we would do most other New Year's. Everyone had brought some food or drink, and we passed the time talking, and then singing. Considering the incredible amount of musicality in the room, it was surprising how many verses to songs we forgot, though we did manage our way through *Homeward Bound* and *Falling in Love with You*, to name a few. Frank was quiet most of the evening, his breath labored, and at certain points we thought that this might be his last night. Rita did rouse him a few times, and seeing us he would draw the words "my friends" from within.

Of the people in the room that evening, all knew Frank longer and more intimately than I did. Before he became sick, I had probably met Frank but a dozen times or so, usually at a large function with many of the same people there on this New Year's Eve. That Frank and I became friends during this time in his life is nothing but a miracle to me, for my experience with those who are dying is that they usually withdraw inward. Had Frank done that, I would never have had the absolute joy in being his friend. In honesty, I was always surprised at how Frank valued my friendship, which really had started with an impromptu visit during one of his hospital stays. But once Frank claimed you as a friend, you were blessed with that title, no matter how unworthy you might feel.

The evening was another testament to Frank's friendship to me, and to us all. For, in spite of his pain, Frank was truly a witness to faith, and present in life amid his suffering. I also see now, though couldn't at that time, what New Year's Eve represents. It is the liminal period between the old year and the one to come. However unrecognizable it is, we all live at some level on that cusp: between our world of memory and the uncertainty of the one to come. On this particular evening, serenading our brother, we saw Frank, and all the good memories of him, placed against a future without his physical presence. More than that though, we saw that evening how suffering and pain could not diminish in Frank the sweet expectation of the world to come.

I have always enjoyed New Year's Eve. From a child staying up late to watch *Yellow Submarine*, to a twenty-something seeing the sun rise on the way home, to sharing my children's happiness the first time they watched the ball drop in Times Square on TV. There is something absolutely joyful to me about the prospect of the new: the true antidote to the limitations of the old. Spending that night with Frank, and having seen him live through his illness with such a profound trust and grace, I see how blessed I was to be there then, and for the all too few years before it, when Frank embraced me as his friend. It is anything but odd that one of the New Year's I will cherish most was this past one, for the simple joy of sharing it with Frank.

I Had a Fraternity and His Name Was Frank

Susan L. Fields

May 29, 2015

Some years ago, after having stayed at home with my kids for ten years, I went back to work. It was financially necessary. At first only part-time, but even part-time meant I would change my weekly school of community meeting. I left the "mom" Wednesday morning School of Community and joined another (for convenience), which met in my neighborhood on Thursday nights. Frank was leading. Frank is my brother-in-law and while we had had many conversations in the past, our friendship became more concrete in the School of Community. We spoke often after meetings, I think almost every week. He would call me and say, "It's really important to me. I would go, pray, and read even if no one else showed up. I don't want to scandalize you, but it's more important to me than going to church." As you know, Frank has quite a story: drugs, homelessness, ten years living on the street before meeting and marrying my sister.

So we talked after School of Community about the school of community. It was during this these conversations that I spoke to him about my desire to belong to a small fraternity group. I had belonged to a small fraternity group and that group ended. But I still had the desire to follow the indication to belong to one. At the time I did not think it, but in retrospect, it (the belonging) was for me defined by the form, the formalism: the meeting on such and such a night, read the indicated text, pray the prayer. But I didn't think I was that way. I didn't think I was that way at the time.

I think these conversations were a provocation for Frank. He asked a lot of questions. He had a lot of comments. He too had belonged to a small fraternity group. "I'm not interested in meetings. What's the difference between school of community and fraternity? We already have a meeting, but I want to be open." I'm not sure I had any good answers but it continued to come up in conversation.

It was during one of these conversations that I realized he had been thinking about the "fraternity" issue in a much deeper way. One day he suddenly said, "Ok, I will be in a fraternity with you." And from then on he called me his "secret fraternity sister." Whenever he greeted me it was, "Suzy Wooz, How's my secret fraternity sister?" Not much changed except that we spoke more often. If I had a problem or concern, he followed up. When I get stressed, I get insomnia. Frank worked nights. He told me, "Call me when that happens. You know I'm awake."

He commented on experiences we had together. Frank started to go to the CL summer vacations. He had acrophobia but wanted to follow the gestures and went on the big hike anyway. At the top of the mountain he became very affected. I offered to walk back down with him. No big deal. We walked back down together, got to the bottom, looked up and waved to everyone at the top. Many, many times he commented to me about how much it meant to him to be accompanied.

He bought a new car and came to my house to show me. "I know this is not a big deal for most people," he said, "but when I think of where I came from, and where I am now, I'm real proud. I changed. I wanted to show you because it's more than the car."

I changed jobs. I started to work full-time. It was a very difficult job and in many ways went badly. I worked in the administration and was to become director of a soup kitchen and women's shelter—a place Frank knew well as, during his time on the streets, he had eaten there often. Getting through that job was a real New York story, a navigational nightmare. Frank was there with an insight I did not have. I have never been homeless. There were objective difficulties at this job and injustices, terrible injustices. Frank was a rock. He was able to judge the situation. I just couldn't. With his companionship, with his clarity, I remained in a tough situation until I changed jobs.

From time to time, my sense of "formalism" crept in. I would ask Frank about inviting people into our group, and having meetings. Frank had this facial expression that communicated a mix between discomfort and irritation. "I don't feel obligated to do that," he'd say. "That's not what this is for me." One year after I came home from the fraternity exercises (Frank could not go because of work), I called him and said, "You know, we need a prayer. Something simple. We just pray it every day for the intention of our fraternity." "Ok, that's cool."

"Whatever you want; it can be the Our Father."

So it was the Our Father. It was his prayer of preference. He called me almost daily, "Yo, Suzy Wooz, Let's do it!" Later, we would pray the *Angelus*.

Over the course of our little fraternity, many, many events took place. My brother Paul was in a near fatal car accident. My sister Mary was diagnosed with brain cancer and died 10 months later. Frank was diagnosed with cancer. He called me. I remember exactly where I was when I received that phone call, under the elevated train walking down New Utrecht Avenue in Brooklyn. "I'm gonna beat this!" he said. I cried.

And life went on. Our little fraternity started to grow. Maurizio [Capuzzo], Rita and Jonathan joined. Maurizio took a job in California. Frank called me and told me. He said, "I know we will still be friends. I'm certain of that, but when I get into bed at night and I hold my wife in my arms, it's different."

Frank's illness progressed. He remained very, very positive. I took a new job and went back to school, first receiving two certificates, then enrolling in a master's program. Frank fought his illness. I started a job in Long Island City, Queens. I left home every day on the 6:31 a.m. train and arrived at 36th Street in Queens usually at 7:25 a.m., and walked ten minutes to my job. Usually between 7:30 and 7:35 my phone rang, "Yo, Suzy Wooz, Let's do it!"

I went to see Frank at his home on December 8th. He had had a difficult setback. I walked into his bedroom. Rita was sitting on the opposite side of the bed and said, "Your secret fraternity sister is here to see you." There are moments in time when you realize a separation is coming. All the facts point to it, but somehow you're never prepared. That night, entering that room, looking at Frank, fully conscious looking at me, I wept and wept and wept. The more I wept, the more irritated he became, "Come on Suzy, we can talk about this."

"I can't," I said.

After, my sister and I sat together at their dining room table, "I'm so sorry," I said, over and over again, "I just wasn't prepared."

"It's ok," she said. "He has to realize what's really happening."

I started to call Rita on my morning walk to work, "How's it going," I said.

"Hard," she replied.

My mother came and went for extended periods in these last few months, then my sister Regina came to help and care and decide. As a family we had been through the drill before. It was time to make some decisions. Eventually he went to Calvary hospice, in the hospital ten blocks from my house. I could walk there to see him. Proximity is a big deal in New York City. Frank rallied (as my father and sister before him had rallied). I cancelled the winter semester classes I had signed up for and went to see him as often as possible after work. Family came. Friends came. One day as I walked into his room, he looked up and said, "Yo, Suzy Wooz, I've been thinking a lot about you."

"You have," I said.

"Yes," he said, "because you're following. Not many people would take the risks you're taking. You're going back to school. You found something you love."

Listening to him speak to me as if it was the beginning, as if he wasn't really dying, as if his participation in life, in my life, was going to continue, was just a marvel. It was comfortable. It was familiar. It was a gift, and I knew it. Sometimes during these visits Frank cried a lot, "Take care of my kids," he said.

"Okay," I said.

Sometimes we laughed. "Yo, Suzy do you have a razor blade?"

"I'm not giving you a razor blade."

"Com'on Suzy, you know you can trust me."

"It's not a problem of trust. You're on morphine. It's not safe."

"Then give me that straw."

"Okay." He cleaned his nails.

"Oh," I said, "I'm really glad I didn't give you the razor blade."

Frank died on January 19th in the early morning. I still take the 6:31 train every morning. As my foot falls on 36th Avenue in Long Island City and I pass the Key Food on my right, come to the curb to cross the street, I start to list all the things that need to be done: what I need to accomplish, materials to prepare for my students, articles to download and print to read for class, bills to pay, my own children's needs, my husband's job difficulties, and then, as I look at my phone, I have this acute awareness that it is not going to ring, that I will not hear that familiar call, "Yo, Suzy Wooz, Let's do it." That first moment I'm incredulous, "How can this be?" The second moment is prayer, the *Angelus*.

Made in the USA
Monee, IL
26 March 2023

30553451R00166